MIKE RANDALL

The Funny Side of the Street

BLOOMSBURY

First published 1988
Copyright © 1988 by Mike Randall

Bloomsbury Publishing Ltd, 2 Soho Square, London W1V 5DE

British Library Cataloguing in Publication Data

Randall, Mike
    The funny side of the street.
    1. Journalism——England——London
    History——20th century
    I. Title
    070'.92'4   PN5129.L6

    ISBN 0–7475–0086–X

    Printed in Great Britain by
Biddles Ltd, Guildford and King's Lynn

From his first day in journalism nearly fifty years ago, when he put the wrong caption on a picture of Deanna Durbin, Mike Randall's career has been one of dizzying ups and downs. Naturally he enjoyed an exhilarating view from the heights when he was named 'Journalist of the Year' for 1965 and congruently the *Daily Mail,* which he edited, was deemed 'Newspaper of the Year' by 'What the Papers Say'. But scaling and slipping down slopes can be diverting as well – as long as you keep your sense of humour. 'When the editor's cup runneth over,' warns Randall, 'you can be sure that a time bomb ticketh under his chair.' Few could claim so long-standing a close acquaintance with Fleet Street as it was – its parade of characters, whiz-kids and tyrants, its pressure-points and watering holes. From papers now laid to rest like the *Daily Sketch, Sunday Graphic* and *News Chronicle* to the birth of the *Glasgow Sunday Standard* – with the *Daily Mirror, Daily Mail* and *Sunday Times* in between – Randall does not mince words about the curious dynamics of policies and personalities that have boosted and undermined circulation figures.

He discusses the creative art of filling out expenses sheets (and why they should begin, 'bus fare to Putney'), he gives guidelines to the beneficial and detrimental consumption of alcohol in the line of duty and explains why Wilson and Macmillan were the best ministerial drinkers. He recalls the mysterious pitfalls of weekending with Viscount Rothermere in the Cotswolds, lunching with the Queen at Buckingham Palace and trying to get a decision out of Harold Evans anywhere but in the *Sunday Times* men's lavatory.

Unapologetic in his appreciation of chauffeur-driven cars and his own window table at the Ritz, Randall also learned the consolations of mushroom farming and even the dole when times got rough. Fleet Street as we knew it may be no longer, but with convivial and entertaining veterans like Mike Randall we can be delighted that the memories linger on.

**FOR GERALDINE,
MY TRUEST FRIEND EVER**

Contents

Preface   viii

Acknowledgements   x

1   Daylesford Dilemma   1

2   Deep Purple   11

3   Coronation Cavalcade   28

4   In the *Mirror*   40

5   Chronicle of Despair   52

6   Christmas Is Coming   63

7   In the Chair   74

8   The Ritzy Life   86

9   Word Perfect   96

10   Court Circles   108

11   1966 – and All That   116

12   Hurricane Harold   128

13   Enter Maxwell   145

14   Agricultural Interlude   151

15   Ninety-Day Wonder   160

16   Excuse Me ...   171

Preface

Nigh on forty-eight years ago a young ex-clerk with no journalistic training entered a London newspaper office and took his seat at a smoke-hazy table where he was to be initiated into the art of caption writing. All that was required of him on his first day was that he should scribble a score of words to accompany a picture of an actress. Despite committing a major error of fact in this, his first, attempt at Fleet Street journalism, he thereafter climbed, step by bizarre step, to the top of his profession and down again.

I was that caption writer. Nearly half a century later I look back on the funny side of the street that still leads from the Strand to Ludgate Circus but no longer spews out its nightly torrent of (mostly bad) tidings. Walk down Fleet Street today and you will not encounter a jostle of journalists or see the scuttling vans carrying their loads of bundled papers to the main-line stations. The great titles have gone, or are going, to the new heartlands of computerised newspapers – Wapping, the Isle of Dogs, Battersea or Kensington. The last to go will be the *Daily Mail*, founded in 1896 and the first paper to reach a circulation of one million copies a day. Early next year the *Mail* will move to the old Barker's building in Kensington.

To be cartographically accurate, the Fleet Street that is no more never was. I contrived to be a 'Fleet Street journalist' for thirty-eight years, working for seven different national titles, without once entering an office that stood on the short thoroughfare squeezed between the Temple and the City. My career began in Gray's Inn Road (the *Daily Sketch, Sunday Graphic, Sunday Chronicle*), continued in Fetter Lane (*Daily Mirror*) and took me via Bouverie Street (*News Chronicle*) and Tudor Street (*Daily Mail*) back to Gray's Inn Road (*Sunday Times*). But I was never far from the journalists' favourite watering holes which are now presumably frequented by the Big Bang society as the City takes over the street.

Were this a serious book I would lay the blame for the exodus on newspaper managements and printing unions equally. But this is not the place for a post-mortem on the death of the last great manufacturing industry in inner London.

Fleet Street has gone and only memories remain. Here are mine, strictly without tears.

Mike Randall, January 1988

Acknowledgements

Great gratitude is due to Gerry Cortese for her valuable advice and sustaining encouragement; to George Johnson and Paul Rossiter of the *Daily Mail* Library and the staffs of the British Museum Newspaper Library at Colindale and the *Daily Mirror* Library for their unstinting help in my research; to Barbara Randall for correcting my errant memory and my grammar; to Liz Calder and Sarah-Jane Forder at Bloomsbury and Reg Davis-Poynter, my agent, for their helping hands; and to the many generous people who have contributed anecdotally to these pages (listed in order of their appearance): Neville Randall, Ian Jack, Keith Waterhouse, Geoffrey Goodman, Bill Hicks, Tom Baistow, Charles Widdup, Arthur Butler, Bernard Levin, Anne Robinson, Don Berry, Lewis Chester, Cal McCrystal, Michael Ward, John Ryan and Ronald Harker. A brief version of one of the events in Chapter 1 first appeared in *The Times*.

1

Daylesford Dilemma

Until the year of our Press Lord, 1961, my only knowledge of Daylesford, the Cotswold home of the late Viscount Rothermere, proprietor of Associated Newspapers, was contained in seven blunt words from William Hardcastle, my predecessor as editor of the *Daily Mail*. 'Enough to make you a bloody Communist,' growled Bill when I asked him to describe his first weekend as a guest of our noble boss.

Bill Hardcastle, a superb newsman, whose life was brutally taken from him at the peak of his achievement in revolutionising BBC radio news in his 'World at One' programme, left many marks on the *Daily Mail*. They were to be found on the legs of his massive desk where he stubbed out most of the eighty Chesterfield cigarettes he smoked each day.

In August 1961 it was my turn for the Daylesford début. As Bill's deputy I was, for the first time, editing the paper during his absence on holiday and one of my daily duties was to report progress on the phone to Lord Rothermere. I had worked for him for nearly four years but I knew little more about him than the strength of his handshake, so seldom had we met. Whether or not he liked the sound of my voice on the phone or thought he should take a closer look at the man now running his paper I do not know, but a sudden summons to Moreton-in-Marsh was delivered on a Thursday night. I was to arrive at Daylesford on Saturday in time for lunch and, by command of His Lordship's social secretary, bring with me a dinner jacket, swimming trunks, a lounge suit and a country suit. I did not have a country suit. I was not even sure what the landed gentry meant by a country suit. Nor did I know which ready-to-wear tailoring firm in London could cope with a man who was 6 foot $2\frac{1}{2}$ inches tall, weighed ten and a half stone, had a stoop (caused by the constant expectation of a stab in the back) and a head which, when it emerged from the womb, was not set on to the body at the correct angle.

My first call next morning was at Simpsons in Piccadilly, where a perplexed salesman said: 'It's not exactly that you are grotesque, sir, but do you drive a car a lot and are you often hunched over your desk? ... Yes, I thought so. I'm sorry, sir, there's really nothing I can do. You'll never be a ready-made figure and don't let anybody anywhere ever sell you a ready-made suit.' With that admonishment he managed to make me feel even worse than I normally do when I have to expose my freakish figure on a crowded Mediterranean beach on the first day of a holiday. (I now have a secret list of foreign beaches where your nearest neighbour will be hundreds of yards away.)

I drove to the office and asked the social secretary if I could get by with spongebaggers (well-cut trousers with mini checks) and a smart jacket. 'Certainly not,' she snapped. 'You must have a country suit.'

In some alarm I called our adroit advertising manager, Jack Reeves, to an urgent conference. 'Don't worry, Mike,' said Jack, laughing indulgently at what he clearly regarded as a paltry problem. 'Can you take a long lunch break?' – a totally unnecessary question since I had long ago mastered the art of extending the lunch hour to its furthest limits.

At 12.30 I climbed into the back of Jack's chauffeur-driven Jaguar and we headed for Gieves, where the reaction was a rather less blunt repetition of the Simpsons scene. Retiring hurt, we decided that a solution to the problem might well come over a leisurely lunch at the Caprice, in Arlington Street. Leaving the restaurant in a buoyant state of wine-induced optimism, we put ourselves in the hands of Messrs Airey and Wheeler, only to be rebuffed with: 'I'm sorry, sir, but we just do not cater for a man of your size and, er, unusual shape, if I may say so.'

I was now in no mood for a fourth opinion and told Jack I was going back to the office to produce the paper and Rother-mere would damned well have to put up with my spongebaggers. 'Don't worry, Mike,' said Jack, 'I've got another idea.'

Immersed in the paper, I forgot all about country suits until, at 4.30, a man from Hector Powe arrived in my office with seven of them. There was one which, while it did not conform completely to my figure, did not appear to be trying to get away from me. Even so, urgent alterations were needed. 'If you can have it ready by 6.30,' I said to the unperturbed salesman, 'I'll buy it.' Next morning I drove to Daylesford in a grey Prince of Wales check with a touch of blue. It was my forty-second birthday and I was, as I quite often have been, between marriages. But I was to make subsequent visits as a married man and my wife was always invited.

There were pitfalls for guests unused to the Rothermere lifestyle. His timetable was rigid and he could not conceal his annoyance if you were five minutes late for the pre-dinner dry martinis. Yet, on going up to change on the first evening of a weekend visit, you would find that, while your wife's dress was laid out on the four-poster bed, your dinner jacket was nowhere to be seen. In a moment of panic your finger hovered over the bell-push you knew you dared not touch. If you went down in a lounge suit, should you say you forgot to pack the dinner jacket or confess you could not find it?

Given time and luck you would find the compulsory dinner jacket laid out in another bedroom across the passage, where the bed was also turned down. Were you meant to sleep apart? Or did your host think you had brought your mistress and was he indicating that discretion was called for? To the country-house habitués it was presumably no problem. They would have known that the second bedroom was simply the man's dressing room. And it would not have taken them twenty-four hours to realise that, further down the passage, there was a second bathroom for the man's exclusive use. But Marmaduke Hussey, then a director of Associated Newspapers and now chairman of the governors of the BBC, confessed to me that on his first visit he went to bed in his dressing room, crept out of it when the house was quiet and joined his wife, only to creep back again before the breakfast tray arrived.

There was also the loo-paper puzzle in your private bathroom. Beside the comfortably contoured lavatory seat stood an antique pedestal table; on the table, a china plate; on the plate the sheets of toilet paper laid out fanwise, each sheet overlapping its neighbour to within one-eighth of an inch, the whole design being, from my observation, restored to its patterned perfection twice every twenty-four hours. Envisage the problem for the enquiring employee-guest: how to lift that china plate, turn it over and inspect the pedigree on its underside, firmly grasping the paper the while, so that he would not be crawling round the bathroom retrieving dropped sheets when the manservant came to lay out the dinner jacket. It was worth the risk: the plate was Dresden.

There are mere millionaires and there are rich millionaires like Lord Rothermere. Ask him how many bedrooms there were at Daylesford and he would simply reply: 'Enough.' I have slept in three of them, each with its individual colour scheme. The breakfast china always matched the curtains and bedspread and the face towels were changed every time you used them.

Daylesford was built by Warren Hastings on his return from India at the end of the eighteenth century. And Rothermere's Hastingsmania was one of his more engaging extravagances. He once discovered that there had been, in Hastings's time, a rose garden on a hill. The exact spot in the grounds where it had bloomed was now flat and roseless. No problem. Summon the bulldozers. Order the bushes. And there, on your next visit, is the hill of 1,000 roses.

Among my Daylesford memories are the following scenarios:

After the Bloody Marys, as the guests assemble in the dining room for lunch, enter two flunkeys, each carrying a plate. Plates are handed to His Lordship, flunkeys fling open the French windows, Lord Rothermere steps into the garden accompanied by his two dachshunds and gives them their lunch.

At dinner: Rothermere to the chief woman guest: 'My dear, I'm so glad you like this champagne. I've just laid down two thousand dozen'; Rothermere to me: 'Nonsense, Randall, of course you can eat some more. What you must do is to take six deep, slow breaths and you'll find you can start again.'

After dinner: Rothermere on the phone to his housekeeper: 'I've just realised tomorrow is the twelfth. There will be grouse for dinner, I trust? And Mr Randall would like sausages and bacon for breakfast. *Have* we any sausages?'; Rothermere, wearing a green velvet jacket with black lapels, his feet clad in dark blue slippers with a gold R and a crest, discoursing on public schools: 'I went to Eton in the days when it was made so tough and Spartan for us that we were all supposed to turn out as fine Empah Wallahs. Thanks to that system, of course, we've lost the entire Empire. Why do you suppose the British behaved as they did in the colonies? Simply because if you are beaten and bullied all the time at public school you've got to go and take it out on somebody afterwards.'

At Daylesford one of the most bizarre episodes in my professional life was enacted, one in which I took no active part. The year was 1964. Four months before the General Election I had agreed with Bernard Levin that he should have a 450-word column five days a week in the *Daily Mail*. On 2 June I wrote to Rothermere explaining that the column would be wide-ranging, tackling only one subject at a time. I continued: 'One would not expect it, nor I think wish it, to conform to everything else in the paper. It would obviously have a radical streak of thought running through it and this, I feel, would be no bad thing come the autumn.' This proposition was in keeping with what I had written to Rothermere in April 1963, when I, a

Labour voter, was appointed editor of his Tory paper. My letter said, in part:

I believe we are agreed that politically the *Daily Mail*, while being a paper of the Right and a supporter of the Tories, will not make the mistake of upholding the outdated ideas of outdated men; will not assume that everything Tory is good and everything Labour is bad; will welcome new thinking and new men from whatever quarter; will not shut its columns to those who oppose its policies; will not take up automatic political attitudes to events ... will remember that its prime function is to be a service to the community and will aim to put the country's interests before any one faction.

Bill Hardcastle had begun to liberalise the absurdly Right Tory line of the paper and I was determined to continue the process, opening our columns to viewpoints unfamiliar to regular readers of the leading article which then appeared in the first column of the front page, where it stood stolidly firm on its Right foundations. I once asked its distinguished author for more than thirty years, the late George Murray, OBE, if he would ever voluntarily write a leader that contained one word of praise for Labour, in or out of office. He replied: 'Good God, no. Who do you think I am?' But he was a professional and allowed me to incline his column at least a few inches to the Left. We became firm friends in the process.

Bernard Levin wrote four or five specimen columns for Rothermere who, verbally, agreed that we could inflict Bernard on our readers. As was his cautious custom, Rothermere put nothing in writing but Bernard, with a nod and a wink from me, drew up his contract. There have been few, if any, contracts like it in Fleet Street. It read, in part:

Clause One: All interpretations of this agreement, together with any dispute, disagreement, difficulty or difference of opinion regarding it, shall be discussed and resolved in a spirit of mutual goodwill and esteem on both sides, with plenty of give-and-take and constant expressions by both parties of their admiration for the talents and capacities of the other.

Clause Seven: Each and every one of the articles shall be well and choicely written, full of wise saws and modern instances, and a credit to the paper in which it appears. Bernard Levin further undertakes to be tractable and sweet-tempered at all times, and to co-operate fully in the production of the column, save that it is agreed that when he is suffering from insomnia and hay-fever he shall be entitled, while continuing to fulfil all other provisions of this agreement, to act like a bear with a sore head.

Clause Nine: Should any article be in its tenor or views contrary to the known and declared policy of the *Daily Mail*, this shall not in itself constitute a reason for its not being published, though the *Daily Mail* shall at all times be free to indicate, in an appropriate manner, that the views expressed by Bernard Levin are his, and are not necessarily or in fact those of the *Daily Mail*. None the less, the editor of the *Daily Mail* shall have the right to reject any article in its entirety. It is, however, agreed that this right shall never be exercised capriciously or unreasonably, and its possible exercise will in every case (if any) be discussed first with Bernard Levin, provided the latter is both available and sober, in which connection Associated Newspapers shall make every effort to get in touch with him and he shall make every effort to become sober if he is not.

Clause Fourteen: Should Bernard Levin be prevented by illness, accident or other *force majeure* from writing the articles, the agreement shall stand as if he were continuing to write them. But if he shall fail to write any article, or fail to ensure delivery of it in time for publication, for any other reason (such as laziness, forgetfulness, inability to think of a subject, intoxication, silken dalliance or the like) Associated Newspapers shall be entitled to reduce its payments to him under this agreement by a sum of twenty pounds for each such article ...

On 29 June 1964 the first Levin column appeared, with this opening paragraph: 'These have been vintage days for students of lunacy. In Southern Rhodesia, an African demonstrator who threw stones at a police dog was promptly shot dead, thus indicating that somebody had taken rather too literally Madame Roland's dictum: "The more I see of men, the more I admire dogs." '

Students of the fantastic were also about to gather vintage material. During the General Election campaign Bernard asked me if he could write four consecutive columns, the first three to be examinations of the Tory, Labour and Liberal policies and personalities; the fourth to be published on polling day and to be a personal explanation of why Bernard would vote Tory/ Labour/Liberal. On the morning of Thursday, 15 October, Bernard duly explained (without my foreknowledge) why he would, albeit reluctantly, vote Labour. He did so in a manner more convincing and in prose more eloquent than the *Daily Mail* leader writer could muster for his customary and predictable 'Vote Tory' article on page one. Here are the closing Levin paragraphs:

In the quiet of the polling booth, the last truth will not be silent: we dare not RISK another Conservative administration, nor trust them to do what they have so conspicuously failed to do in thirteen years – to carry out the radical transformation of our country – its economics, its education, its social structure – that Britain must have if Britain is to be saved, and help save others.

The Conservatives, both in men and ideas, are exhausted, and there is no possibility of their regeneration while they are led as they are at present. I think it is time to make this clear. Let's go.

What dire things were said at Daylesford when Lord Rothermere heard the news that Harold Wilson was in with a four-seat majority, I have yet to discover. But his reaction was instant and drastic and the sequel was, for me, a near disaster, a black comedy, a miracle, a farce, or any permutation of the four.

It was the custom that anyone from the office visiting Rothermere for the weekend should report to his London secretary and collect whatever letters, publications or parcels were awaited at Daylesford. That post-election weekend Bob Hammond, then managing director of Associated Newspapers, followed custom and spotted, among the envelopes he had to take, one, as he told me later, 'with familiar handwriting on it'. He did not read the name and address but thought it must be important and placed it on top of the pile. Arriving at Daylesford before lunch on the Saturday and finding, not unusually, that his host was out with the dogs, Bob Hammond deposited his deliveries on a sitting-room table and waited. When Rothermere returned and had poured the drinks, Bob Hammond said: 'I've brought your letters from London. The one on top of the pile looks important.'

Rothermere went to the table, picked up the envelope, looked at it and strode back to Hammond saying, 'This is for you,' and left the room. Hammond picked up the letter which was indeed addressed to him in Rothermere's handwriting, was marked urgent and had originally been delivered by hand from Daylesford to the London office.

Hammond opened the letter and, to his consternation, read this:

Dear H.

For the first time in the history of Associated Newspapers a member of the editorial staff has given his political opinions in the columns of the *Daily Mail* without the consent of or even the knowledge of the Proprietor. Such an event is intolerable and demands the resignation of everyone concerned in the matter. I would remind you that when I saw the editor of the *Daily Mail* in the board room in your presence I told him that the *Daily Mail* had to support the Tories not only in the leading article but also throughout the newspaper. My instructions have been flouted and I am not prepared to tolerate such action.

Yours sincerely
R.

By the time Bob Hammond had digested the letter and decided on a policy of silence, Rothermere returned and the two sat down to lunch. No mention of the letter at that meal, no mention of it that afternoon on the customary walk in Daylesford's ample acres, nor during the customary swim in Daylesford's indoor pool ('always keep the temperature at seventy-eight'), nor at dinner, nor all next day until, at last, shortly before Hammond was due to drive back to London, he turned to Rothermere and said: 'That letter. Shall I deal with it in my way?'

'Yes,' said Rothermere – and that was all he said.

Bob Hammond's way was to send for me and ask me not to do it again. Nothing was said at the time to Bernard Levin whose contract, which Rothermere had never seen, made it impossible for anyone to demand his resignation for expressing, however forcefully, political opinions contrary to those of the proprietor.

We can only guess at Rothermere's motive for the letter. Possibly somebody convinced him that, but for Bernard Levin and the *Mail*, Harold Wilson would not have scraped through to No. 10. A most improbable theory, but even the possibility was enough, perhaps, to drive a volatile Press baron, who was a liberal man at heart and did not wear comfortably the clothes of a Tory proprietor, into instant action and hasty regret. It was a clue to the humanity lying just below the protective skin which had grown, I suspect, out of shyness and a well-founded mistrust of people. For a rich millionaire, let alone the proprietor of a newspaper empire, it cannot be easy to distinguish friends from opportunists.

I do not remember being either shocked or upset by the strange event, or non-event. Nor did I take it as the familiar writing on the editor's wall. Surviving it, I felt somehow more secure in the editor's chair. How, without any obvious qualifications, I reached that chair will be revealed in the ensuing chapters of accidents.

2

Deep Purple

War and waning health led me accidentally to Fleet Street. Son of a commercial traveller in corsets (he did not wear them, he sold them), I was required as a boy to listen to my father reading aloud the staunchly Tory leading articles in the *Daily Express* in the days when they often began with 'Halleluiah!' and went on to praise all the Right things. I was sent to preparatory and public boarding schools, the fees being paid, at some sacrifice, by my long-suffering mother whose slender independent means also had to cope with father's drink bills. When I left public school, at seventeen, having attained Higher Certificate in French, German and subsidiary English (A-levels to most of my readers) and been turned down by an Oxford college, my mother, who by then had left father and was running a boarding house in London, somehow managed to send me to France and Germany (six months in each country), allegedly to study. My subsequent fluency in both languages was due more to my falling in love than to the scant attention I paid to professors in Montpellier or Freiburg im Breisgau. But all my life I have been grateful for that experience.

Back home, at eighteen, it was time to start work. My first interview was with the British American Tobacco Company, where an aloof man in a pinstriped suit informed me that I was not suitable material to send to China, though he declined to say why. After that rejection my new stepfather (my mother having by now married my former prep school headmaster) decided that I should 'have my bumps read'. That meant going to the National Institute of Industrial Psychology, where I was given an IQ test (which, with its spot-the-odd-man-out approach, I have always regarded as the easiest of exams and one which proves nothing). That led, for no logical reason, to my taking a clerking job in the City, despite my total inability to cope with mathematics. I joined a firm of import-export merchants, sat on a high stool, made the directors' tea, wrestled with the old-fashioned telephone switchboard, frequently pulling out the wrong plugs, and was paid 17s 6d a week.

In 1939, when I was twenty, I was posted to the firm's Rio de Janeiro office where I inexpertly handled bills of lading and other baffling trade documents. Most of them ended with the warning 'E and OE' ('Errors and Omissions Excepted'), which seemed at the time to be a blanket excuse for my many mistakes. Later in life I came to think that the same disclaimer should appear at the bottom of the back page of every newspaper. By some incomprehensible decree from Whitehall my clerking chores were classified as a 'reserved occupation', meaning that I was not required for military service. My firm was not willing to send me home and it was with some difficulty that I eventually persuaded the British Consul, on whose good-will my return journey depended, that I could be better employed in the Army than in facilitating the entry into Brazil of large quantities of British gin.

In the winter of 1940, when the Battle of the River Plate had rid the South Atlantic of the German battleship *Graf Spee,* I at last took passage in a merchant ship bound for Liverpool. We sailed in convoy, passengers nervously sharing watches on the bridge as submarine-spotters, but saw no sign of the enemy during the six-week voyage. Back home, the Army rated their new recruit as zero. A combination of the aftermath of severe yellow jaundice (my Rio doctor diagnosed it in its early stages as VD, insisting that all young Englishmen in Brazil caught it) and the emergence of an ulcer in my duodenum (where, according to my Irish doctor in London, it would remain until I was forty-five, and mature − a state I have incidentally not yet reached even though the ulcer has gone) caused the military medical board to reject me outright.

Out of uniform, out of work, out of money, I wrote to Sydney Carroll, founder of the Regent's Park Open Air Theatre and then editor of the now defunct *Daily Sketch* (it will emerge from these pages that I have worked for as many deceased organs of opinion as I have for existing newspapers). My brother Neville, who later became a distinguished feature writer but is probably best known as the researcher/scriptwriter of the popular 'Focus on Fact' strip which ran in the *Daily Mail* until his retirement, had been working for Carroll before he temporarily exchanged the pen for the sword. Neville got his chance in Fleet Street (via Oxford and Pitman's) when he was told, in an interview with a *Sketch* executive, that his undergraduate writings were rubbish and that he should go away and do a piece under the absurd headline: WHAT STOCKBROKERS EAT FOR LUNCH. Fortunately we lived next door to a broker who ate sandwiches every day at the ABC milk bar, which gave Neville what is known in the trade as a good angle − and a job on the *Sketch*.

Chronology will now give way to anecdote; here is Neville's story of his favourite interview with a celebrity:

In 1955 almost everyone who had a television set switched on to the BBC's top panel game, 'What's My Line?', to watch an erudite, witty, rude and testy member of the panel called Gilbert Harding. They were waiting for his temperature to rise above its low boiling point and the explosion which would hit the headlines in the papers next morning.

When my editor, Bertie Gunn, ordered me to interview him and make him account for his nationwide notoriety, it was an unwelcome assignment. I phoned expecting a caustic refusal. I was surprised by a courteous invitation to present myself at nine the next morning.

At the start of a steamy August day in that scorching summer, I rang the bell of his flat near Tottenham Court Road and braced myself for a peppery reception. Another surprise awaited me. The door was opened by his manservant. From his bedroom door, Harding emerged in his dressing gown and led the way to the bathroom. I was offered a seat on the bathroom stool. Harding disrobed and clambered into a well-filled hot bath. The manservant reappeared to place a tray on another stool. On it were two wine glasses and a newly opened bottle of Pouilly-Fumé 1953. He poured a glass for each of us and withdrew. Harding took a gulp and began to talk.

'It all started in 1947,' he said. 'No one had heard of Harding then. I had tried my hand at schoolmaster, policeman, journalist and lawyer. A wartime job with the BBC in Canada was coming to an end. I was nearly forty and unknown. I returned to Britain to find myself jobless.'

As he talked and plied me with wine, I realised that I would not have to ask him any questions. Once launched on an autobiographical tide, he swept through the story of his rise to fame with a flow of succinct sentences, pausing only to sip the wine:

'The BBC was reducing its staff. The jobs I wanted other people got. The jobs they offered me I didn't want. The North American Service lent me to Talks. Talks didn't think I had the placidity and patience for them. They lent me to the Light [programme]. Norman Collins was looking for a chairman for a new programme called "Round Britain Quiz". They thought I was an intelligent gasbag. It wasn't what I wanted. I wanted a regular job with security, office hours, PAYE and a pension. Instead I was unestablished.

'"You're a broadcaster," they told me, "not a staff man." I pleaded to be a broadcaster on the staff, even at half the freelance rates. "If you're a freelance," they smiled, "we can sack you. If you're on the staff, we have to find you another job." They added kindly: "We want you from time to time. But not all the time, brother."

'They were the most terrible words I've ever heard. I was faced with spending the rest of my life hanging round the pub waiting to pick up jobs. And so, with appalling dismay, I left the staff of the BBC on 1 April 1948.'

Jobs were thereafter showered on him by radio producers: 'Round Britain Quiz', then 'The Brains Trust'. Before he had time to visit the BBC pub he found himself on 'Twenty Questions' and 'We Beg to Differ'. Then television bagged him to join the panel on 'What's My Line?'

Harding took a cigarette to brace himself for the effort of dressing and to reflect on his luck. Between puffs he relaxed as his manservant pulled socks over his feet, which a succession of celebrity dinners prevented him from reaching without strain.

'What's My Line?', he confessed, 'turned me into a public notoriety, bringing with it the advantages, and disadvantages, of bazaar openings, speechmaking, sponsoring pens, and all the paraphernalia of phoney publicity.'

Now, he explained, he could pick his celebrity appearances all over the country and name his own fee. No one wanted Harding till he got the sack. Then no one could do without him. How did it happen?

'Getting the sack,' he mused, 'was the incentive to work more than office hours. But the change is the reflection of the low standard of public taste rather than a reflection on me. It's a mystery. One of the people I like least is me. I can find nothing which will explain why the rest of Britain likes me. The descent from success will be sharp, severe and painful.'

The interview was over. It was not long before his forecast was fulfilled. Leaving the BBC, he collapsed with a heart attack and died. Of all the celebrities I have interviewed, no one, I felt, had bared his soul – or his body – more completely than Gilbert Harding. I wish there had been more like him.

To resume the narrative, my 1940 letter to Sydney Carroll made the outrageous claim that anything Neville could do I could do better, although my only published writing was five lines which had appeared in *Punch*, on that opening page which used to contain a topical collection of quirky quips under the headline LONDON CHARIVARIA. Within days I was summoned to a 6 p.m. interview with Carroll at Kemsley House in Gray's Inn Road. He told me to go home and write 600 words about Rio. Since the only thing I knew about newspapers was that they were in constant competition with the clock, I decided that the article must be on Carroll's desk before he arrived at his office next morning. It was – and I was hired as a caption writer (who produces the words under the pictures and the headlines above them) at £4 a week. I was entering the only truly classless society I have ever known. Nobody on newspapers cares about where you come from, what your accent or your clothes are like, where you were educated or who your parents were. Prove that you can do the job and you are accepted. And such was my luck that for the next thirty-seven years, although I worked for many different newspapers, I never had to apply for a job. The offers came to me and, rightly or wrongly, I was always reluctant to say no.

In 1940 the *Daily Sketch* published scores of pictures every night and we caption writers, clustered round a table in a haze of cigarette and pipe smoke, would have a procession of prints flung at us with instructions to fill a certain word space. Each photograph was supposed to have enough information on the back of it to enable us to do a quick rewrite, but the information was often minimal. On my first night the first picture thrown at me had two words on the back – Deanna Durbin. I filled the required space, but next morning readers were ringing in to ask when and where they could see the film in which the *Sketch* said Deanna was starring. Alas for me, the film had not been made – and never has. I cannot recall how I came to make the error but I was soon forgiven and went on to write 10,000 or more captions.

For me the job was a nightly pleasure. Whereas sub-editors invariably had to condense the news stories they handled, caption writers frequently had to expand their subject matter to fill the allotted space, allowing us to write as best we could. We did not produce great prose (a tall order when you have only a few minutes for composition) but we strove for passable English. One art I never mastered was the writing of captions for 'cheesecake' pictures, those photographs of pretty but scantily clad girls who appear in popular papers for no newsworthy reason but are presumably published for the pleasure of a male-dominated staff in need of light relief. Years later (and long before the *Sun*, under Rupert Murdoch's ownership, adopted the 'Forward with the Nipple' policy) I explained my dilemma in a 1967 'What the Papers Say' programme for Granada television. Here is an extract from the transcript:

I was stumped whenever I was given a picture like this ['cheesecake'] and told to write 100 words with little to go on but the girl's name. You cannot just write down the first thoughts the picture arouses in your mind, can you? So let us see how today's expert caption writers cope. First, the breathless caption (in the *Daily Mirror*):

'Here's something to make any civil servant crash his forms-in-triplicate on to his desk and stare! For lovely nineteen-year-old Venettia Matania was once a £9-a-week civil servant herself. Until she became a £70-a-week belly dancer. For a "moving" view of her, see Anglia TV's production "The Crossfire".'

Next, the *People*'s way:

'It could be said that Donna Marlowe-Reading jumped from the rag trade into the slave trade. She started her working career as a fashion model. But Donna, eighteen, was soon spotted by film and TV people ... When she's not busily occupied in her dual roles as film and TV actress, she's probably cooling off in London's Roehampton pool.'

Now for the *Sunday Mirror*, explaining the presence of their Sunday girl:

'Intelligent. Easy on the eye. Co-operative. In fact Hollywood actress Cami Sebring is so co-operative she didn't even raise a lovely eyebrow when the photographer said: "I want you to pose in a leopard-skin bikini, lying on your left side with your right arm behind your head." She could justifiably have said: "Oh, no! Not that!" Taken all round Cami would make a pretty nice "big" sister. But a much nicer girlfriend.'

My prize went to the *News of the World*:

'Beautiful 24-year-old Carole Rhyra has just arrived at London's Raymond's Revuebar with some distracting statistics and a unique in-laws problem. "My husband, Gino," she said, "is an Italian but his family haven't been able to see my torrid love scenes in a new French picture. It's been banned in Italy. It's not fair." So she's brought a stage act over here "because my boss, Paul Raymond, and the English are so broadminded".'

Inanity, inanity, when newspapers parade female flesh, all is inanity.

In 1941 I wanted to get married, an impossibility on £4 a week, so I doubled my money by moving down two floors after my Friday shift on the *Sketch* and putting in a stint on the *Sunday Graphic* (long since deceased), another Kemsley publication dominated by pictures. Finishing at about midnight, I would return on Saturday morning and work two more shifts. That equivalent of an eight-day week may not have been the best working arrangement for a new husband, but financially it provided a vast bedsit in Kensington and a bearded Irish cleaning lady. It also put me on the path to an editor's chair.

After I had worked casually for the *Sunday Graphic* for a few months, the editor, Reginald Simpson, a florid, bull-necked man who was known to his staff as 'Deep Purple' (because of the colour he turned whenever he lost his temper, which was at least a dozen times a day), asked me why I had not applied for the permanent job of deputy art editor. I reminded him that there was no such post on his paper. 'Don't be such an effing young fool,' roared Reg, 'I've just created it.'

It was impossible to resist such a pressing invitation, and I joined the staff of the *Sunday Graphic*. There I encountered a string of eccentric characters, among them Dennis Dunn, the humorous writer who was sacked because Simpson disliked the hat he insisted on wearing in the office; Jimmy Spencer, the deputy editor (later editor of the *Liverpool Post*), whose main duty at the busiest time of the week was to clean Simpson's Home Guard boots; John Drummond, wounded RAF rear-gunner who, posted to the Ministry of Information which allowed him to do a Saturday reporting shift for us, delighted in biting secretaries' necks; Group Captain Leonard Cheshire, VC, the bomber pilot hero who wanted to put the world to rights through his writings; the Rev. W. H. Elliott, who wanted to cleanse the world of its many sins; C. B. Fry, the great cricketer, whose sports copy was written in laborious longhand; A. P. Herbert, who delivered his weekly verse by telephone; and Jacko Gordge, the art editor, who typically rendered himself speechless with laughter when he produced for a film review the headline TOO MANY DEAD MEN ON BOB HOPE'S CHEST (the critic, Helen Fletcher, having protested in her article that there was too much comedy about corpses in Hope's latest film, *The Princess and the Private*). He later capped that with TOO MUCH ARSENIC, NOT ENOUGH OLD LACE, which speaks for itself to those who recall the book and the film.

Not all headlines came as easily as that. The outpourings of the Rev. Elliott were a weekly tribulation to even the best of sub-editors and the headline problem was usually solved by the group method, three or four of us suggesting, rejecting, tossing ideas back and forth – and sometimes nipping across the road to the Blue Lion for a glass of inspiration.

In January 1945, when the end of the war was in prospect and spirits were rising, the Rev. writer chose to open his column with: 'This *is* a very, very sick world. To pretend that it is not is to lie impiously before God and man.' He then went on to berate his readers for the slump in their ideals, for which, he declared, the only cure was faith in God. What headline could possibly make a war-weary public read such a message at such a time? Fortunately Elliott had included in his article a form of spiritual quiz designed to show how faithless we all were, thus enabling us to dodge the issue of faith and present his piece as EIGHT QUESTIONS THAT MUST BE ANSWERED, hoping that a few readers would persist after the first paragraph.

Simpson had a mania for labelling all the regular features. We had 'Enid Blyton's Corner' (a somewhat nauseating piece for children, retailing the adventures of a sickly-sweet character called Pip the Pixie, known to the staff as Pip the Fornicating Pixie), 'Spotlight on America' (by Paul Gallico), 'I Go to the

Pictures' (by Helen Fletcher), 'A Nature Picture Story' (by Frances Pitt, who endlessly wrote about, and photographed, the animal world), and 'Today's Talking Picture' (a label that Simpson would put above the front-page photograph after he had discarded all my suggested headlines and failed to write one himself).

When Jeanne Heal joined the paper on 7 January 1945, Simpson suffered his worst bout of labelitis. This was hardly surprising when Miss Heal began her first article (under the label 'A New Feature Mostly for Women') with these puzzling words: 'Don't be under a misapprehension – this isn't purely a woman's column. What is a woman's column anyway? It's surely a mistake to think that women are interested only in their own affairs. Anything interesting is, I say, a woman's interest. So here goes.' And there she went, meandering on about bread, knitting wool, glycerine in cosmetics, plastic materials, collapsible tables, coffee-brewing, perms and fluorescent powder.

So what is a woman's column? If Miss Heal did not know, neither, apparently, did Simpson. By 21 January 'Mostly for Women' had become 'Mainly for Women'. By 28 January, it was 'Our Feature for Women'. By 11 February it was 'Our Woman Columnist's News-Feature'. By 18 February Simpson had given up the struggle and the label was simply 'By Jeanne Heal'.

One of the pleasantest but sometimes most exacting tasks was to take A. P. Herbert's Saturday-morning phone call when he dictated his topical verses from wherever he happened to be (more often than not it sounded like a pub). During the war A. P. H. was skipper of a patrol vessel on the Thames. The reason he had to phone in with his compositions so close to press time is best given in his own words, extracted from an article he wrote on the fifth anniversary of his first contribution to the *Graphic*:

On Friday morning, when I turn out, my crew in the *Water Gypsy* are accustomed to hear a hollow groan. 'O Lord! Any suggestions?'

Nothing happens until I go ashore on Friday evening. Then I puzzle and scribble away between bites or beers. With luck I finish the job in my bunk at midnight.

Then there is the problem of communication. On Saturday morning I might be at Tilbury or, further still, in Sea Reach. Riverside phones are rare down there and people who want to bawl long passages of verse to London are not very welcome.

In 1940 and '41 my record nearly went on many a Saturday morning after a bad blitz. I remember vividly the little dark passage at the dear old Lobster Snack at Canvey Island – dogs barking, sailors 'ranting and roaring' in the bar next door, people tumbling over my feet. And I was yelling down a very faint line: ' "How is the old Top Wop today?" T for Tommy – O for Orange – P for Percy – *Top!* Now, *Wop!* What? *Wop! Wop! Italian!* W for William – O for Orange –' and so on throughout the whole composition.

All these years I have never seen a proof. There is no time. We make a check over the telephone and hope for the best.

And his hopes were justified. Searching through the *Sunday Graphic* files I could find no example of an error of transmission, hazardous though it was. But I did find this, which, when A.P.H. wrote it in March 1945, echoed my sentiments at the time.

Technical Hitch

'I beg your pardon for the slight delay
In half a minute Mr Smith will play.
Meanwhile, here is a record I commend –
Though it may have to stop before the end.'

O Lord, to what a bondage have we come!
Not for a second may the air be dumb!
And men apologise with abject words
If silence falls and we can hear the birds.

We were a somewhat unruly crew on the *Graphic*, a natural reaction to the verbal scorn that was daily poured on us by our editor. But we were kept in order by Ted Mosedale, the head printer, who could not tolerate the slightest incompetence in journalists. When one of his men accidentally dropped the metal type of the 'What the Stars Foretell' feature all over the composing-room floor and nobody could find the original copy, Ted turned to the nearest journalist and barked: 'Better write some forecasts yourself and do it bloody fast.' I did – and foretold a happy day for everybody.

One Saturday afternoon I was in the editor's office, trying to persuade him to withdraw his order to rewrite half the captions in a picture page that was urgently wanted in the press room, when our altercation was interrupted by an internal phone call from Mosedale whose every word I could hear as he bellowed into his mouthpiece. There ensued the following exchange (in language which was perfectly normal in newspaper offices in those days):

MOSEDALE (to Simpson): 'That bloody banner headline you sent me for the front page. The bugger has bust by one letter [meaning that it was one letter too long for the space allowed].

SIMPSON: Don't be so damned stupid, Ted. I tell you I wrote and counted it myself and it bloody well fits.

MOSEDALE: And I'm telling you the bloody thing's bust and I want another one fast.

SIMPSON: Don't give me that bloody rubbish. Set the fucking thing again.

Simpson slammed down the phone. Seconds later Mosedale burst into Simpson's office and dumped on his desk the heavy lump of hot metal (old technology) which was the offending headline. 'If you say that'll fit,' roared Mosedale, 'you'd better set the fucking thing yourself.' And he stormed out.

Defeated, Simpson turned to me and snapped: 'Write another headline, Mike. You've got one minute.'

'But what about this page we were discussing?' I asked.

'Send it to press, you fool,' he said.

Simpson threw ink bottles at his secretary before taking her to dine at the Savoy, appeared to prefer dogs to humans, tore up the fruits of hours of our labour just to keep us on our toes, and regularly demanded the impossible from his staff. One morning at conference, at the height of the war when almost everything was rationed, he was kneading a pile of pipe tobacco on his desk. Turning to John Ralph, the news editor, he said, 'Get me a story about the disgraceful shortage of tobacco. Find out what's being done about it.'

'But, sir,' pleaded John, 'there's a war on.'

'I know there's a bloody war on,' said Simpson, 'but I want to know why I couldn't get any tobacco at my local shop this morning. Don't argue. Go and find out.'

Needless to say, nothing appeared in print. For all his faults, Simpson was a good editor and knew when to draw back.

Few of us could have endured the Simpson regime if we had not kept our sense of humour. One afternoon, towards the end of a horse-steak lunch in nearby Hatton Gardens, then the home of diamond merchants who traded on the street, one of our photographers passed round our group a tiny piece of glass. We huddled in a circle, closely examining what fellow diners clearly thought was a diamond. We earnestly discussed its value and then, as we were leaving, the photographer pretended to drop the precious object. We scrambled about in search of it but eventually, giving it up as lost and loudly proclaiming that it must have gone down the drainhole, we abandoned it. Returning to the scene fifteen minutes later, we were rewarded by the sight of diamond merchants on their hands and knees searching the area which had now been cordoned off.

Back at the office, Simpson was in his familiar deep purple mood. He had decided that Frances Pitt's nature notes should this week be projected as a whole page of pictures, featuring a rabbit. It had fallen to me to write the captions and, to relieve the tedium caused by having in the past few months written captions for CRAZY JANE THE SPINSTER WILD DUCK, CAT MOTHERS WILD RABBIT, MY FAMILY OF OTTERS AND TINY THE TERRIER, THE VANISHING BITTERN, THE FAITHLESS GANDER, MY FOSTER FOX CUB, THE TERN IN A TANTRUM, THE ACROBATIC STARLING and CAT MOTHERS A WILD RAT, I had chosen to write these captions in verse. Further, they were to be reproduced in white on black which, technically, meant that once they were transformed into metal not a line could be changed. When the page proof landed on his desk, Simpson yelled for the art editor.

'Jacko,' he spluttered, 'who wrote this bloody crap?'

'Randall,' replied Jacko, 'and I like it.'

'Tell Randall that A. P. Herbert writes the verse around here, and he can do this damned lot again – in prose.'

With that Simpson took up his blue pencil and put a cross through the page. Jacko emerged ashen-faced from the editor's office and gave me the bad news. This time it was more than my colleagues could stomach. Three of them marched into Simpson's office where they demanded, and got, a retraction.

In 1946 Simpson put two dogs on the staff of the *Sunday Graphic*. Our new colleagues, naturally treated with greater favour than the rest of us, were a couple of bob-tailed, traffic-trained sheepdogs called Bobs and Chips. Simpson had seen a picture of them doing their master's shopping and crossing the road at a Belisha beacon. He asked the owner to call, signed up the dogs immediately and launched them on a series of road safety demonstrations for children. In a few weeks they were famous and schools were clamouring for them. We never found out how much Simpson paid them, but we suspected their salaries were more generous than ours.

Blunt as Simpson's methods were, there was no faster way of learning the trade than by working for him. It was on a Saturday night that he promoted me to features editor, ordering me to take over at once a department of which I had scant knowledge. Three weeks later Simpson was appointed editor of the *Sunday Chronicle* (another now defunct Kemsley paper) and decided to take me with him. A few days before we moved offices he sent for the *Chronicle* staff list and, without waiting to meet any of them, put his blue pencil through some twenty names. 'They're all fired,' he announced. 'Got to show the buggers who's the boss.' Unfortunately the National Union of Journalists was at that time a comparatively powerless body and its officials were unable to save all the members so callously dismissed.

But it was not long before Simpson followed them out of the building. The transfer from a picture tabloid to a text broadsheet was one he never mastered. His bullying tactics continued, as exemplified by his treatment of my deputy, Barbara Thomson, a talented sub and reporter from the *Eastern Daily Press*. When he sent the smartly dressed Barbara to cover the Wimbledon fashion scene he was delighted to see her pictured in the *Evening Standard* wearing a particularly attractive hat. 'Just the kind of girl we want on the *Chronicle*,' he told me. But when he discovered she was a Labour supporter he insisted on sending her to cover all the meetings of the Housewives' League, a group whose attitude she disliked and of whom she could not write the required adulatory reports. 'Bloody little Red' was how Simpson now described her.

Perhaps the last straw for Barbara was when Simpson bought the serial rights of a distasteful book called *Duel in the Sun* (known to the staff as *Lust in the Dust*). Barbara and I had to edit it into instalments. We expressed our disapproval by including in the first instalment all the bluest bits in the early chapters. Presented with the galley proofs, Simpson made a deep purple exit from the office and spent half the night re-editing the extract to make it suitable for a 'family paper'. When we faced the expected wrath next morning Barbara decided it was time to quit. The minimum notice for staff wishing to leave was one month but she found a short cut. In her letter of resignation she wrote: 'I can no longer work with enthusiasm for an editor for whom I have so little respect.' As soon as Simpson read it he banned her from the office forthwith – with a month's salary.

Simpson's own departure was as sudden. We believed he was having an affair with a girl in the wire room, whence copy was dispatched to our Manchester office. Be that as it may, one Saturday night he left the office, drunk and dishevelled, with his arm round the girl. He was spotted by a management man who reported the episode to Lord Kemsley. That was the last we saw of Deep Purple.

Thereafter we had three editors in quick succession. The first was James McDowall, a distinguished war correspondent suffering from a punctuation mania which caused him to spend hours poring over proofs in search of misplaced commas. It was under his editorship that I was given my first unwelcome taste of back-stabbing. I was one of the lecturers for the Kemsley training scheme and my subject was layout. It was my habit to take with me to the lectures a few examples, drawn up by myself, of how not to design a page. At the end of the lecture I would consign these dud layouts to the nearest wastepaper basket, not bothering to tear them up. After one such lecture a fellow executive, who undoubtedly wanted to oust me from my job as features editor, retrieved my examples of bad design from the wastepaper basket and took them to the editor with the comment: 'I thought you ought to see the kind of pages Randall would produce if I didn't persuade him to change them.' Fortunately, the plotter was unmasked and exiled to our Sheffield office. But my friends sent a warning ahead of him and he was soon out of newspapers and into public relations.

McDowall was succeeded by Sydney Carroll (formerly of the *Sketch*) of whom legend has it that he probed into Lord Kemsley's background with such devastating effect that he was able to put on His Lordship's desk the manuscript of a proposed

book with the challenge: 'Would you like to see that published?'
From then on, so the story goes, Carroll could have a job in the
Kemsley empire whenever he wanted one. On the *Chronicle*
Carroll initiated an agony column, the blurb for which was
aimed at attracting way-out sexual deviants. Carroll kept all
the unpublishable letters locked in his desk. I know, because I
found them there after his departure.

Carroll's successor was the genial, talented Scot, Gordon
McKenzie, who had the curious habit of banging his head
against the wall, hoping thereby to produce brilliant ideas for
feature articles. Small wonder he was frequently escorted home
suffering from severe migraine. I became his deputy and it was
probably through McKenzie, who had the ear of our editorial
director, C.D. (now Sir Denis) Hamilton, to whom he had
previously been personal assistant, that I was unexpectedly
offered the editorship of the *Sunday Graphic*. To Hamilton's
surprise, I pleaded for time to think it over. He did not know
that I had quietly been planning to give up journalism and enter
the oil world.

3

Coronation Cavalcade

Play me a Judy Garland record and my thoughts will filter back to my old friend John Drummond, a scatty Scot and the aforementioned biter of the backs of secretaries' necks. He had by now abandoned journalism and joined the sober-suited ranks of the Shell company. Much as he loved to work with words, massaging them into free-flowing sentences, happy as he was at the typewriter, he had, with his unbounded enthusiasm for all forms of life, fathered six children by his early thirties and decided, for their sake, to put business before pleasure. His last post in journalism was dramatic critic of the *Sunday Chronicle* and one of the assignments I gave him led to a bizarre interview with the still-lamented Judy, a singer for whom we shared a passion, and whose voice could simultaneously melt our hearts and fan our fantasies.

Drummond had spent most of a tedious day trying to keep the various appointments Judy had made with him, only to be told each time on arrival that the star was resting, or in conference, or unwell and would he call later. At about 5.30 p.m. an exasperated dramatic critic, who had obviously resorted to whisky to relieve his frustration, returned to the office to warn me that the space I had reserved for his article was likely to become a gaping hole unless I quickly organised an alternative piece. I said I would accompany him that evening to the London Palladium, where Judy was nightly enslaving her audience. I phoned my wife to ask her to abandon the cooking but prepare the sofa for an overnight, and probably overwrought, visitor (is it at all surprising that journalists are near the top of the divorce league?), and we set off, via the nearest pub, for the footlights.

By the time we reached the theatre Drummond was tipsy; by the time we had fortified ourselves with two quick ones in the interval he was sozzled. In that state, at curtain fall, he wove his way to Judy's dressing room, myself in tow. I made no attempt to restrain him because I knew of his remarkable and enviable ability, by exercising extraordinary mental discipline, to sober up when the occasion demanded. No doubt emboldened by the whisky, but in the most articulate manner, he began by berating Judy as a callous, selfish, ill-mannered, inconsiderate bitch for the treatment she had meted out to him that day. The great Garland, who was lying on her couch and was also in a less than sober state, at first ordered her henchman to throw us out. Then, pouring herself another drink, she recanted and gave forth a string of usable quotes, expletives deleted.

What I had not foreseen was that Drummond, who had taken no notes but accepted yet another whisky, was instantly re-intoxicated the moment he left the dressing room. I took him to my home where, on putting him to bed, I discovered he could not remember one word of the interview. When I set off for the office next morning he was in a deep sleep. I left beside the sofa a hastily scrawled version of what I remembered Judy saying and hoped for the best while preparing for the worst. A few hours later my fears were allayed when Drummond phoned in with enough competent copy to fill the space. Poor Judy. As Ronald Neame, who directed her in her last film, *I Could Go On Singing*, recalled in an interview only last year: 'She was not allowed to grow up. From the age of eight she lived in the studio. She was driven there and back in a limousine and never did the things that growing up people do. As a result, she could no more buy herself an airline ticket than she could fly the plane.'

It was Drummond who persuaded me to apply for a post in the Shell public relations department. He argued that if I could get through the first few months of the grim contrast between the free-and-easy camaraderie of a newspaper office and the highly disciplined ways of a big firm (I would even be compelled to arrive at the office in a hat, which I did not possess) I could scale the Shell heights and emerge, as he eventually did, with the kind of fat pension which in those days no journalist could expect.

It was on a Friday that Denis Hamilton offered me the editorship of the *Sunday Graphic*, giving me the weekend to decide. I had not yet had my first interview with the relevant Shell director, and I knew that if I passed that test I would still not be accepted until the company's doctors had declared me fit. There seemed no way to vault those two hurdles between Friday night and Tuesday morning, when Sunday paper staff begin work and I would have to give Hamilton my answer. I put the problem to Drummond who, ever the trained journalist, persuaded the Shell director to break with company tradition and interview me at his home on Sunday. He said the job was mine subject to a medical test the next day. That night I celebrated, in no half-hearted manner, the beginning of a new life.

When, on Monday morning, the Shell doctors had completed their examinations, one of them came to me and quietly uttered the chilling words: 'We think you should see your own doctor immediately.'

'What on earth for?' I protested.

'We think you have diabetes,' was the awesome reply.

Drummond and I rang round our medical contacts and within a few hours I was consulting a leading diabetic specialist in Harley Street.

'Did you drink much last night?' he asked with a chuckle.

'A fair amount,' I said. 'I was celebrating.'

'It was what the whisky did to you that fooled the Shell

doctors,' he said. 'You most certainly do not have diabetes.'

The consultant wrote a strongly worded letter to the Shell medicos, refuting their findings and declaring me free of all symptoms of diabetes. I delivered it by hand and went home to await the response. When the director phoned he explained apologetically but firmly that the company rule was that if the Shell doctors said you had diabetes then that was what you had, no matter who might say otherwise. It was a rule that could never be waived and, since it meant that I could not qualify for the pension scheme, I could not join the staff. QED.

Next morning, having been warned that I would be on trial for three months, I accepted the editorship of the *Sunday Graphic*. The year was 1953 and I was thirty-three. I had not shaped the events which propelled me from trainee caption writer to the editor's chair in thirteen years; chance had put me there and chance was to remove me nine months later. In the meantime I had two immediate problems: the first was how to transform a pedestrian paper, which, because of its cramped and airless layout, made little impact on the reader who idly turned its pages, into a product which was bright enough to the eye to fasten the reader's attention on as many items as possible; the second was how to cope with the unnerving silences of Denis Hamilton. The first was solved in a week; the second took a little longer.

In newspapers there are trained designers who will dazzle you with modules, laterals, symmetricals, asymmetricals, verticals and horizontals, and there are the rest of us who, having visual minds, design by instinct. Let that fine writer Ian Jack, former member of the *Sunday Times* features team (which he joined from the Scottish *Daily Express* 'where none of us had been inside an art school but threw together pages which conveyed a crude excitement and played havoc with the grammar of typography'), describe in his own words how the high priests of planning perform:

On the *Sunday Times* feature pages every headline-size and illustration had first to be pondered gravely by the men and women of the design room and then transmitted to the printers via page plans which had been drawn up with the help of T-squares and different colours of ink. It was as though we were producing aero-engines.

The chief designer, Edwin Taylor, spoke in opaque metaphors and stroked his moustache. He had guru status. One day, shortly after I found myself in charge of the women's pages, we went to lunch. My section was called 'Look!' and the discussion over whether we should retain or abolish that exclamation mark lasted through a bottle of retsina. Eventually Edwin said: 'The trick with the "Look!" pages is this. Imagine molten chocolate pouring down from the wooden deck of a ship. It's not the bits that stick in the cracks between the planks you've got to worry about, it's the chocolate that falls through into the hold.'

'Eh?' said I.

'Well,' said Edwin, 'try it another way. Imagine you're a Zeppelin flying over London in 1918 ...'

I never discovered what we had been talking about.

My instinctive design method was, I trust, more comprehensible. I was later to describe it for Harold Evans when, as editor of the *Sunday Times*, he compiled his five-volume *Manual of English, Typography and Layout*. I was by then managing editor (news) of the *Sunday Times* and far removed from the tabloid flippancies of my formative years in Fleet Street. My contribution to Volume Five was:

I take the sheet of layout paper. It is $15\frac{3}{8}$ inches wide and 22 inches deep. I pencil in the ads. I read the copy. I am hoping to capture the writer's mood, to be certain about his emphasis, to be in tune with his copy. And I am looking for a headline. When you are lucky, when mood and headline come together in exciting conjunction, your enthusiasm rises and your creative instincts get the necessary adrenalin. I look at the pictures. I see the headline visually. It may be a running headline (a long one) or it may be a stark, big three-word headline. Whatever it is, I make the type fit the headline and not the headline the type. Now the page begins to take the shape that I dictate and not the shape that is sometimes dictated by a list of contents which have to be accommodated without sufficient consideration of why and how. In brief, if the words are good I am moulded by them. I feel I must care for them, nurse them, protect them, and then give them the presentation they deserve. If the words are bad, good presentation can make them look a little better. You may thus fool yourself and your colleagues, but you will not fool the readers.

There was another sentence in the original version of that contribution. It revealed that, whenever I was hopelessly stuck for a headline, I would leave my desk and, whether nature demanded it or not, sit on the nearest loo and contemplate. Invariably I thus flushed out the headline I was seeking. But Harold Evans, for all his radical, crusading zeal, was still something of a prude. He put his censor's pen through that disclosure. There was also a half-truth in what I wrote for Evans. You *can* fool some of the readers some of the time and I blush to recall how I did it during my brief reign at the *Sunday Graphic*.

It was Coronation year when I took over. Royal fervour, fanned by the media, spread its glow over the land and, with five months to go until the Abbey extravaganza on 2 June, we on the *Graphic*, in search of rising circulation, barefacedly exploited to the full the national mood, leaving behind us a trail of trivia and an abundance of absurdities. We mounted a continuing feature labelled 'Coronation Cavalcade'. We hired Hector Bolitho, author of *Their Majesties* and *A Century of British Monarchy*, Margaret Saville, author of *Royal Heritage*, and Cyril Hankinson, editor of *Debrett*. There was impact in the layout, but oh! the words.

These were the headlines and subheadings on Margaret Saville's opening salvo: HUNDRED AND ONE PROBLEMS THE QUEEN FACES – *What make-up should she use? Which hairstyle will be the best? What about the horse? Where will the children be? Which shoes for the Abbey?* The article that followed contained this intimate revelation: 'She and her husband will spend long hours beside a log fire talking over the smallest details.' Week after week we paraded our cavalcade of commonplaces. On 29 March the whole of the front page was devoted to a 25-year-old picture which we had unearthed and now proudly presented as an 'exclusive'. It was taken at Balmoral in 1928 and showed the Queen (not quite in focus), aged two, toddling along in the grounds, her hands clasped in those of Queen Mary and the then Duchess of York (now the Queen Mother). Inside the same issue we carried a five-page tribute, in words and pictures, to Queen Mary, who had died a few days before publication. Pray do not call me to account for allowing these lines, written by A. P. Herbert as an epitaph, to appear in the public print:

> *Three words like stars of ancient fame*
> *Signs of the saintly, strong, serene*
> *Shine brighter now, beloved dame,*
> *The words are 'Mary' – 'Mother' – 'Queen'.*

The awful truth is that by these methods we did increase the sales of the paper and, in March, my trial period over, I was confirmed as editor. By now I had worked for Lord Kemsley for thirteen years but never met him. I was summoned by him to a boardroom lunch, attended by fellow editors in the Kemsley group and members of the directorate whose hands I shook for the first time. As lunch neared its end, Lord Kemsley stood up, looked round the table and said: 'Gentlemen, here we have Mr Randall, our new editor. It would be interesting to see if anyone present can remember how many editors the *Sunday Graphic* has had in the last fifteen years.' There was a ripple of that restrained, seemly laughter which a touch-your-forelock body of men deems a suitable response to a proprietor's joke, and they started to count. But they all, including Kemsley, lost count, failing to remember either names or numbers. Ronnie Hogg, then a newsdesk executive, told me recently that in those days 'the *Graphic* changed editors like some people change underpants'. Even he could not recall the total.

Thus encouraged by Kemsley, whom I was never to meet again, I returned to my office and the royal business in hand. Our readers were soon to learn that the Queen would need a special perm to support the Crown, that there were three sizes of soap for Palace guests (small tablets for a two-day stay, large square tablets for a week's stay and two big blocks for long-term visitors), and that sixteen years before, on the morning of King George VI's coronation, an SOS from the Palace had been answered by Cyril Wilkinson, the royal ear-piercer. Queen Mary had been unable to insert her ear-rings because she had disobeyed Wilkinson's instructions and allowed the holes in her ears to become stopped up.

Worse was to follow. Columnist Jeanne Heal discovered 'Mrs Coronation', the title she gave to the wife of David Eccles, Minister of Works and stage manager of the royal show; and the Rev. Frank Martin, who had taken over the god-spot, cried: 'Is the New Elizabethan Age, which is so full of promise in many directions, likely to see a great revival of belief?' He called on his readers to follow the Queen's example of 'deep personal faith' and ended his exhortation with: 'If organised religion misses this providential bus, there may not be another for a very long time.' They missed the bus, Rev. Frank, and I have yet to see the queues waiting for the next one.

One of the problems of a Sunday paper is that, apart from sport, newsworthy events seldom take place on a Saturday. Coronation Day was 2 June but our next issue was on 7 June. We fell back on *The Crowning Week: Souvenir Edition*. Our title, in white lettering on a blue background, was flanked by E and R in red. The front-page picture was of the Queen, in full regalia, holding sceptre and orb. Inside we presented 'Eight Pages to Keep ... for a Lifetime', a regurgitation of highlights of the great day, with such additional titbits as the two-page disclosure by Norman Hartnell, the Queen's dressmaker, of all the secrets of the Coronation gown. A fortnight later we were still suffering from a Coronation hangover. Her Majesty was now on a provincial tour and, on 21 June, we asked in big type on the front page: IS THE QUEEN OVERWORKED? The opening paragraph read: 'All last week the same questions were being asked in countless homes. Is the Queen doing too much? Should she, so soon after the Coronation, have to carry out such a packed and exhausting programme? Surely she must be tired out?'

Challenge me on how we knew such questions were being asked in so many homes and I would have to plead loss of memory but, having thus created anxious readers, we proceeded to comfort them by reporting on 'high authority' (the Palace press office, no doubt) that Her Majesty was in fine fettle and her loyal subjects had no need to worry about her. In the same issue we carried a most improbable feature entitled FASHIONS THE WORLD IS FOLLOWING – SECRETS OF THE QUEEN'S NEW DRESSLINE. I have been terrified by more fashion writers than editors. Being totally incapable of speaking their language, or understanding why they should devote so much space to clothes their readers could not afford, I meekly submitted to their dictates. Our fashion editor on the *Graphic* was Frances Dale, better known to you as the formidable Fanny Craddock of TV cookery fame.

All this royal ranting was accompanied, in our feature pages, by an apparent mania for persuading stage and screen stars to bare their souls:

'DON'T GET ME WRONG,' SAYS DIANA DORS: 'I may be dizzy on the stage but that isn't the real me. Really I'm so quiet and friendly.'

MY REAL SELF, BY HERMIONE GINGOLD: 'I am a complete escapist. I seldom go out in the streets. I haven't seen Oxford

Circus for five years. Tell me, has it changed much?'

WHY I AM BECOMING A NUN, BY JUNE HAVER, the £1,000-a-week Hollywood song and dance star. This confession was followed, eight months later, by WHY I QUIT – June Haver explaining that she left the teaching convent because she was made to work sixteen hours a day and 'I just couldn't take it.'

'I NEVER PROMISE A WOMAN ANYTHING,' SAYS GABLE – which was hardly surprising when you consider what Clark got without promises.

THE RUMOURS ABOUT ME ARE UNTRUE, BY PETULA CLARK: 'I have not got TB. I am not losing weight. I have not had a nervous breakdown.' This was a typical case of Fleet Street backing it both ways. First you spread the rumours, then you cash in by denying them.

'I'M A CHANGED WOMAN NOW,' SAYS RITA HAYWORTH. If only she had been . . .

By the end of my happy-go-lucky editorship of the *Sunday Graphic*, unedifying in retrospect but successful in increasing the paper's sales, I had solved the problem of the sinister silences, the intimidating muteness that so disturbed me at my weekly meetings with the editorial director. I owe two great debts to Denis Hamilton who, having thrust me up the professional ladder, was there to catch me when I tumbled off it. He was a kind but stern man, not quick to befriend, not ready with the words to put you at your ease, but he was such an astute judge of people that he was later, as editor, to handpick the staff who would propel the *Sunday Times* to the pre-eminent position it reached under Lord Thomson's ownership.

Summoned to his office to account for the latest issue of the paper and to be examined on future plans, I would find myself seated opposite a compact, somewhat military figure (he had an impressive Second World War record), sitting in an imposing chair with a back so high that it dwarfed the occupant. Desultory exchanges over, Hamilton would fall silent. At first I thought he was marshalling his thoughts, but when his lips remained sealed for a full ninety seconds (which is a long time in silences) I realised that he was forcing me to do the talking. At such times the victim of this routine is liable to utter the first thing that comes into his head – usually gibberish. He will then be pounced on. After a few months of this technique, and having discussed it with fellow sufferers, I decided to try to put an end to it. When the silence fell at our next meeting, I folded my arms, gazed at the ceiling, surveyed the pictures on the walls, eyed the objects on his desk, scanned the scene through the window behind the high-backed chair – and kept my mouth firmly shut. Finally, there was nothing Hamilton could do but break the silence himself and thereafter he never used the mute method with me.

By that time, a man in Australia was having thoughts that would change my professional course. His name was Hugh (now Lord) Cudlipp, then editorial director of the *Daily Mirror* and *Sunday Pictorial*. While touring Australia he still scrutinised all the London papers and was intrigued by the changes I had wrought in the *Sunday Graphic*. It cannot, I feel, have been the contents that attracted his attention; it must have been the layout. Cudlipp cabled instructions to his London office and, as a result, I received the following abrupt phone call: 'This is Cyril Morton. I work for the *Mirror*. When could we meet for a drink?'

The rendezvous was at Mooney's Irish Bar in Holborn. The Guinness flowed and Morton, who was Cudlipp's favourite fixer at the time, asked me if I would meet his boss and discuss terms for joining the *Mirror*. Never negative in such matters, I agreed. Weeks passed before Cudlipp called for me, but when we met business was concluded in a few minutes. Cudlipp poured the drinks, then asked me what I earned as editor. When I told him (about £3,000 a year plus £6 a week expenses), he burst out with derisory laughter and said he would almost double it if I would become number four on the *Mirror*, with the title of assistant editor, features.

My resignation from the *Graphic* caused Lord Kemsley to ordain that I should never again be allowed to set foot in Kemsley House. I did, but by then it was called Thomson House.

My education in real journalism was about to begin.

4

In the Mirror

If there is an undercurrent of alcohol running through the mainstream of this narrative then I must at once confess that, while I did not owe my survival in journalism entirely to the number of glasses I emptied, they were a mighty prop. While the popular conception of newspapermen as a bunch of Lunchtime O'Boozes is exaggerated, it would be equally wrong to deny that the lifting of elbows plays a part in the creation of newspapers. I speak for my time only and have been informed by normally reliable sources that sobriety is rife among the modern generation of journalists (though even as I was writing this chapter I was invited to lunch in Fleet Street by a senior executive who said: 'Could you make it Tuesday? I'm editing on Wednesday and can't get drunk that day.' The lunch lived up to my highest expectations, including the two bottles of Frascati and the two double liqueurs).

Apart from the lunch break, that blessed interval of indeterminate length between the time when you have gathered your material, or made your dispositions, or theoretically planned your paper, and the time when you have to fill those wide open spaces, there are other moments when instant solace is required. Many journalists live on, and sometimes beyond, their nerves. Whether you are a reporter, news editor, feature writer, subeditor, photographer, night editor or even editor, your harshest master is the clock that cannot be stopped (though I have known the desperate smash its face), the mercilessly moving hands that tell you time is running out and your deadline is nigh.

Meticulous though the preparations may have been for the

coverage of the anticipated events of the day, the unexpected will always throw you off course, demanding immediate re-assignment of staff and re-appraisal of the paper. But the words must still flow, the copy be edited, the page plans completed and the headlines devised – against the clock. To send an edition to press without the latest news, or to cause an edition to miss the train, is the greatest crime. Sweat out your masterpiece of reportage, design your finest page, but what will it avail you if you do not reach your readers at the breakfast table or the station bookstall at the appointed hour? They do not know or care what agonies you have endured. Why should they? They want their paper on time and brook no excuses.

Reporters do not habitually go tight to their typewriters, nor page designers draw their plans with shaking hands, nor editors make vital decisions under the influence. It is when the day (or night) is done and the heart is no longer in the stomach, or vice versa, that the soothing of stretched nerves is essential to the preservation of sanity. That is when the day worker feels the need to repair to the 'outer' office, the pub, to muse over the day's events with colleagues, trying to assess (and a journalist, unlike a politician, has only one chance to get it right) how good a performance has been given.

And I have every reason to know that the night worker at the 1 a.m. finish of a hard stint has scant hope of going straight to bed and enjoying the relief of oblivious sleep. In my night-editing years I would lie there restlessly recreating the problems of the night's labour and wondering if, when I saw the rival papers in the morning, I would find I had been outclassed. What is required may be a stop at the Press Club on the way home, or a tot from the bottle secreted in the desk. I tried the alternative of sleeping pills followed the morning after by pep pills to prepare me for the next night's work. I do not recommend it.

It is true that drink has been the downfall of numerous journalists (and politicians, doctors, authors, scientists and bricklayers, for that matter) but I can testify that controlled drinking has also been the saviour of many. Lest the anti-alcohol cohorts are sharpening their swords, I am not arguing that the first requisite of a journalist is to have a good head for drink. I knew a few teetotallers who proved otherwise. But it would be a dishonest account of the Fleet Street I knew if it ignored the tippling times which, thank heaven, were relished as much by our female colleagues as by us weak males. I cannot abide men-only gatherings.

Journalists can afford their medicinal drinking because they pay for it out of their expense allowances. Expenses are the lifeblood of newspapers, the cure for all journalistic complaints. They are the fillers of empty wallets, the pourers of oil on troubled typewriters, the clearers of writer's block, the restorers of lost confidence. The system is simple: you have typed six different first paragraphs of your story and discarded them all as gibberish. You have decided to seek stimulation by joining your colleagues for a liquid lunch but find you have no money. You grab a form called a 'pink chit' (or 'white lie' or 'swindle sheet', depending on the terminology in your office) and use your imagination to describe on it what assignment you are undertaking (it is wiser to put 'meeting special crime contact re bullion robbery' than 'exclusive interview with Pope'). You then fill in the amount of money you wish to be given in advance, thrust the form under the nose of a busy departmental head who will countersign it without looking, take it to the cashiers, collect the bounty and spend it in the pub.

When the day of reckoning dawns, greater imagination is required (it comes naturally to most journalists) to account for all the money you poured down your throat. You take an expenses sheet on which you itemise your expenditure. You begin modestly with 'bus fare to Putney' and work up to 'lunch with crime informant, bill attached'. You will not, of course, have a bill for that day because you were in the pub, but that is no problem. You borrow one from a colleague who has a large supply of blank bills from his favourite restaurants. You fill in the date, the table number and how many covers. You write food £x and drinks £x (be careful there) and add 12 per cent for gratuities. You then remember that the news editor phoned you that day (he will not recall it but neither will he be able to deny it) and ordered you to get back to the office fast. Hence the next item: 'Taxi from Putney to Fleet Street.' If by now you have failed to account for the total you withdrew in advance, you fall back on desperate devices like 'repair to jacket sleeve torn in rush to get out of taxi to report for urgent assignment' or 'medication for knee injured while running into office and tripping over dislodged paving stone'. Add a few further fictitious phone calls and you are home and dry.

At the end of my first week on the *Mirror* I put in an expense sheet. Since my weekly allowance as editor of the *Sunday Graphic* had been limited to £6, I decided that my new, and more generous, employers would not baulk at £12. Two days later a small cigar-smoking figure burst into my office. Harold Barkworth, the managing editor, agitatedly waved my expense sheet at me. 'Mike,' he said, 'this really won't do.'

'Sorry, Harold,' I replied. 'What shall I cut it down to?'

'Don't be a bloody fool,' he snapped. 'Double it – or else you will be letting the side down by claiming so little.' I did – and thereafter wrote some fine fiction.

The expenses system was ill-suited to some journalists, mainly those who were habitually late with their copy or those whose love-life was in such a tangle that it was draining too much from their wallets and demanding too much of their time. They constantly broke the rule which decreed that you had to account for money drawn in advance within one month of receiving it. Failure to do so would mean that, after being conceded reasonable extra time, you were put on the 'stop list', which barred you from drawing any more money in advance until you had accounted for what you had already spent. If you were an experienced procrastinator, you would then plead that you were on the verge of a scoop which you could not achieve unless you were able to take your informant out to dinner, or that you would have a nervous breakdown unless you could have a holiday. You would be given an extension which would lead you only into deeper financial waters. The hardest case I had to handle, when I was administrator of the *Sunday Times*, was that of a brilliant reporter, who shall be nameless, whose debt to the company had piled up to some £5,000, which included money advanced for foreign travel. When warnings, admonitions and threats had failed, I sent him home and banned him from the office until he had completed the expense sheets which would explain where the money had gone. I knew that the one thing he could not bear was not to have his by-line in the paper and it was no surprise when, within three days, he returned triumphant with a bundle of bills and itemised accounts.

My introduction to the *Daily Mirror* in 1953 was intoxicating. Before I joined, James Eilbeck, whose desk I was to inherit following his promotion to assistant editor, invited me to a Sunday pre-lunch drink. Champagne and caviare awaited me. Then champagne without caviare. Then, 'I think we should open another bottle, don't you?' The more he drank the more the red-haired Eilbeck boasted of his skills and laid so much emphasis on the difficulties of running the features department I was shortly to head that I was seized by an immediate crisis of confidence. Reassurance was not forthcoming when, a few days later, Jack Nener, the *Mirror* editor, gave a welcoming lunch party at which I met the men, all copious consumers of beer or wine, or both, who would be my fellow executives. The benign appearance of Nener, with his thick white hair, was instantly belied by the loud voice which could not (and did not during the three years I worked for him) complete a sentence without a string of crude expletives. There was an occasion during one of those annual political party conferences beside the sea, so tedious that delegates and journalists alike relieve the boredom by propping up bars, when Nener, in full effing flood as he entertained several guests in a hotel restaurant, was interrupted by a man from a neighbouring table who asked him to lower his voice and restrain his foul language.

'Don't you know who I am?' rasped Nener. 'I'm the effing editor of the effing *Daily Mirror*.'

'I rather thought you must be,' said the protester.

Once through the swing doors of Geraldine House, the tiered wedding cake of a building in Fetter Lane which then housed the *Mirror* staff, my fears were dissipated. Here, in a stimulating atmosphere of organised chaos, was a paper with a social conscience; a paper which, though it may have relied largely on its entertainment value for its four-and-a-half million circulation, also ran those dramatic issues in which, page after searing page, it exposed the scandals and espoused the causes of the deprived, the denied and the desperate. Here was a paper which had the honesty when Stalin died and other scribes were blunting their pencils out of false respect for the dead, to come out with the towering front-page headline CROCODILE TEARS and, with rapier words, to denounce the tyrant for his crimes against humanity; a paper which gave space to 'Mirrorscope', a feature which translated the gobbledegook of important but complex developments into simple but accurate language which enabled the layperson not only to understand the subject but also to appreciate its significance. And here was a paper which had, as a separate and little publicised entity, a bureau which gave free, expert advice to those beleaguered by bureaucrats, beset by hounding lawyers, bewildered by civil service jargon or persecuted by landlords.

The instigator, initiator and inspirer was Hugh Cudlipp, editorial director, who instinctively knew what his readers were beefing about. Under him Jack Nener, the foul-mouthed yet benevolent editor who, at the morning-after inquests on the previous night's issue, lashed us for our failings and only occasionally praised us for our successes, was mainly concerned with the hard news coverage (though in my early days he bawled me out for getting the 'Pip, Squeak and Wilfred' strip out of sequence, even though nobody had told me I was responsible for checking it). No matter if Cudlipp and Nener had failed to return from lunch in time for the vital afternoon conference; others were ready to step into their shoes (or read their absent minds) and shape the kind of paper they would have shaped.

And then there was that colossus of columnists, Bill Connor, author of the five-days-a-week 'Cassandra' articles, whose zestful interests ranged from the exploding of hydrogen bombs ('a dress rehearsal for the death of the world') to the construction of shepherd's pie ('like many another homely dish it is not quite as simple as it seems. It can be thrown together. It can be played by ear. But great cooks (I mention no names) prefer to construct it with the precision usually reserved for atomic power stations').

Before I joined the staff, I had been warned that I would have to handle Cassandra's copy and had better beware of this impatient man who did not suffer fools in any way at all, let alone gladly. To my joy, despite the rasping voice and the disturbing way he fixed you with his piercing eyes peering over the rims of his spectacles, we had an instant rapport. When it seemed as if his article was going to be late, I would go to his room, which would be empty save for the litter of discarded first paragraphs lying all over the floor. I would pick them up, read them and know where he was – across the road at Auntie's, sinking a pint or two to release the word blockage. He would soon return and deliver such a piece as this, dated 13 July 1955, on the morning that Ruth Ellis, convicted of shooting her lover in a blaze of vengeance, was due to hang:

It's a fine day for haymaking. A fine day for fishing. A fine day for lolling in the sunshine. And if you feel that way – and I mourn to say that millions of you do – it's a fine day for a hanging.

If you read this before nine o'clock this morning, the last dreadful and obscene preparations for hanging Ruth Ellis will be moving up to their fierce and sickening climax ...

If you read this at nine o'clock then – short of a miracle – you and

I and every man and woman in the land with head to think and heart to feel will, in full responsibility, blot this woman out.

The hands that place the white hood over her head will not be our hands. But the guilt – and guilt there is in all this abominable business – will belong to us as much as to the wretched executioner paid and trained to do the job in accordance with the savage public will.

This was followed by a *Mirror* campaign for the abolition of hanging, culminating in a poll of more than 30,000 of our readers who voted overwhelmingly (20,509 to 11,057) against capital punishment. Yet it was a curious comment on female feelings at the time that, although it was a woman who had just gone to the gallows, more women than men voted for the retention of hanging.

No subject was too vast, or too minor, for treatment by Cassandra's masterly pen-strokes. Here he is, in playful mood, on 21 December 1953:

During the next three days about 350,000,000 Christmas cards will be fired in the British Isles . . . Now I am an old gunner in the Christmas Card Artillery, and it seems to me that more should be known of the military postal science of causing Yuletide mortification, annoyance, irritation, inconvenience, vexation, offence, resentment and deep anger. The whole practice is such a thundering nuisance that it is high time that some practical advantage such as causing unhappiness was extracted out of the wretched business. I think I can point the way . . .

And he did, with a mischievous humour that, alas, probably misfired with many of his readers.

When only fifty-seven, Cass, as we all knew him, died in April 1967, a few months after he had paid me a tribute that I can never forget. But that is for a later chapter.

Keith Waterhouse (of *Billy Liar* and much other subsequent fame) was my senior feature writer. Modest in manner, he was the true professional. I could send for him and say, 'Keith, I have this damned 350-word space to fill. The only subject I can offer you is, frankly, crap. But there's nobody else around at the moment. Can you take it on?'

Keith would suck his pipe, nod his head and say only: 'I see.' But when he returned with his 350 polished words the subject no longer seemed to be crap.

In December 1954 I confessed to him that I could not fill the Christmas Eve issue unless he wrote me a short story of about 1,200 words. Just before Christmas there is a paucity of news, which explains the quizzes, jumbo crosswords, party games, cookery corners and competitions which, dressed up with drawings of holly, mistletoe and ringing bells, fill the festive columns. Keith sucked a little harder on his pipe and produced, at the exact length, a story of his northern childhood which began:

I was eight, nearly nine. They had all this blinking holly and cotton wool and that all over, and we went singing carols, banging on people's doors and going: 'Little bit of spice cake, little bit of cheese, glass of cold water, penny if you please. If you haven't got a penny, a halfpenny will do, if you haven't got a halfpenny your door's going through.'

If those words are familiar it is because that short story was the inspiration for Keith Waterhouse's first of many books, *There Is a Happy Land*, published in 1957. Paragraphs from the *Mirror* story are, in his words, 'spattered all over the book'.

The reporting of events sponsored by your own newspaper is nobody's favourite task. If the spectacle is a flop, how do you disguise it? And if you fail to mention one of the invited celebrities you are in the doghouse. Keith skilfully averted one of the pitfalls when he covered the *Daily Mirror* Pet Dog Parade. Since it was organised by a Paper of the People, it was strictly for mongrels. Five hundred dogs and 42,000 spectators thronged the Festival Pleasure Gardens in London.

Keith reported one shambolic incident in these words: 'The parade had moments of sheer, delicious pandemonium. When the stars appeared – Guy Mitchell, Abbott and Costello, Ted and Andrew Ray, Diana Decker, Eunice Grayson, Elizabeth Allan – about half the kids in the crowd mobbed them for autographs. It took a band and a dozen megaphones to shoo them off.'

So far, so true. The full story is that the band and the film stars were not supposed to converge at the same time, causing utter chaos, and the loudest voice that was heard required no megaphone. It belonged to Jack Nener, who, to the horror of hundreds of *Mirror*-reading dog-lovers, bawled as only he could bawl: 'Get those effing people out of here' – referring, of course, to the invited celebrities.

The day that Keith lays down his pen will be a black one for me, though I doubt that I shall live to see it. And if you would like to know what a good journalist does in his lunch hour(s), consult his 1986 book, *The Theory and Practice of Lunch*, with this opening paragraph: 'I know of only one pleasure of the flesh more acceptable than lunch – and lunch is so perfect a curtain-raiser to it that they make a classic double bill.'

The *Mirror* in the mid 1950s ('The Biggest Daily Sale on Earth') could switch with ease from I MEET CHOU, a potentially important but rather pedestrian account by the then Rt Hon. Harold Wilson, MP, of his meeting with the Chinese premier Chou En-lai, to THE BRA KING WHO SAYS UPLIFT IS MY BREAD AND BUTTER by Marjorie Proops. One of the paper's most prophetic campaigns in 1954 was called THE ROBOT REVOL-UTION, known today as the microchip era. It is remarkable that these words were written thirty-four years ago:

All this week we have been telling you about automation – the Robot Revolution that will change your life. Today we warn the politicians: there must be planning now for the changeover ... Unless there is political planning there will be industrial chaos ...

The Robot Revolution can bring mass happiness or mass despair.

It offers more leisure and less drudgery to working people. But if we go wrong, mass unemployment and the dole queue will be back again.

There was no planning. There was industrial chaos. Mass unemployment is back. More power to the Press!

I was only on the fringes of the *Mirror*'s serious side; my main duty was to provide the entertainment essential to maintain the mass circulation. In that I was aided by a clutch of colourful characters. Pat Doncaster, equally at home at the keyboard of a piano or a typewriter, urged me to persuade Cudlipp to let us mount the first *Daily Mirror* Pop Festival, starring Alma Cogan, Winifred Atwell, Eddie Calvert, Lita Rosa, David Whitfield and Jimmy Young. I recall an evening spent with Jimmy when, convinced that his kind of crooning had outlived its welcome, he sank ever deeper into gloom and painted for himself a black picture of an unemployable has-been. Tell that to the millions who tune into his radio show!

Tony Miles, who joined my staff as a spotty-faced youngster, was to crown his Fleet Street career by becoming chairman of the *Mirror* group. Throw him a headline that asked HOW DO YOU WOO? and he would produce a series of articles that brought in shoals of enthusiastic letters. He also had the strange habit of driving straight across roundabouts.

Donald Zec was the wit who charmed the most intimate secrets out of actresses (he was adept at assisting Kay Kendall with her make-up, selecting the 'Blustery Weather' face lotion and deftly wielding the black pencil to give her a beauty spot before taking her out to lunch). Donald had readers of his column laughing all the way to the cinema.

Noel Whitcomb was the man-about-town columnist. Returning deeply distressed from Ascot one evening, declaring to all and sundry that he had written one of the worst columns ever printed, he stopped me as I was leaving the pub to go home and begged me to talk over his problems – in a nightclub. Noel, still in his Ascot rig, conducted me on a tour of six clubs that night, but neither the champagne nor the hostesses nor the leggy floorshows raised his spirits. When, in the early hours, we made our unsteady way to his Hampstead home, Noel's understanding wife, Sally, produced the necessary coffee and made it clear that she was not going to have a drunken, snoring husband in her bed. There was only one other bed and neither Noel nor I could remember next morning why we had shared it. But Noel's depression had lifted.

In my three years on the *Mirror* I was a constant admirer of Hugh Cudlipp who, more than any one man, moulded and equipped me for what was to come. Yet we never became friends, perhaps because I did not take the trouble to understand his real nature. I was once summoned to his office to find there a bewildered, bearded man, whom I had never met before, sitting awkwardly in an armchair. Cudlipp poured generous drinks as usual (on big news days, like royal weddings, executives would gather in his room for a 10.30 a.m. champagne conference) and turned to me.

'Mike,' he said, 'this is — —. He is a scoundrel, a despicable chap in many ways and a man you cannot trust. But he can write and he is joining your staff – so be warned.'

I was shocked, angry and resentful but, not wanting to prolong the man's agony, escorted him from Cudlipp's office without revealing my feelings. It was only years later that, learning of the writer's past history, I realised that Cudlipp was, in his own peculiar way, doing him a favour by giving him a job at a dark moment in his life.

It was with a typical Cudlippian gesture that I parted company with him. When the time came for me to move on (at my wish, not his) he broke the office rules and gave me a goodbye cheque to which I was not entitled.

It was 1956, the year of Suez, when chance again diverted me. The *News Chronicle* beckoned and, as was my custom, I succumbed.

5

Chronicle of Despair

It used to be a common claim among newspaper people that, since their creative industry bore no relation to, say, the toothpaste or confectionery business, they should be exempt from the harsh economic rules that govern other manufacturers. But the reality is otherwise. While the rank-and-file journalist lives for the moment, knowing that in such an ephemeral trade what is written today is written off tomorrow, it is the duty of management and editor to take the long view of their newspaper. They must constantly plot and re-plot the course to a secure future. My friend Michael Curtis, a brave if over-optimistic editor, had been fighting for two years for the *News Chronicle*'s survival when he asked me to join him, in 1956, and support him with what he flatteringly called my 'technical expertise'. I had tasted real journalism on the *Mirror* and, having acquired an appetite for it, was glad of the chance to abandon my role as an entertainer and be enrolled in the ranks of the radicals.

When Michael Curtis, formerly the chief leader writer, assumed the editorship in 1954 he was warned by his predecessor, Robin Cruikshank, that the paper was already in financial straits and that, in the last resort, Laurence Cadbury, the chairman of the company, would sell out to Lord Rothermere's *Daily Mail*. Cadbury was unlike any other proprietor I ever met. He did not have the arrogance of Cecil King, the *Mirror* chairman who denigrated all who disagreed with him, nor the intuitive flair of King's successor, Hugh Cudlipp, nor the lofty, aristocratic approach of Lord Rothermere, nor the economic shrewdness mixed with beguiling honesty of Lord Thomson, nor the appalling aloofness of Lord Kemsley. A most unfortunate giggle punctuated his conversation more frequently than a writer uses commas, which made it difficult for the listener to take him seriously. It is not true, as some have said, that he giggled while the *News Chronicle* burned, but he unwittingly gave that impression.

Cadbury was not in sympathy with the radical, humanist and liberal traditions of his paper, whose first editor was Charles Dickens. His political preference was for the moderate Conservatives and his favourite paper was the *Daily Mail*. He was also a careful chocolate millionaire. His London flat in a Curzon Street block was chosen because it was near a bus stop that was conveniently on the route to the *News Chronicle*'s Bouverie Street office. It was a service flat to which ample meals would be delivered by the block's restaurant. But I learned from one distinguished guest that if you were invited to dine there your host would announce that the food available from the restaurant was not to his taste and he would cook the meal himself. Donning a waiter's jacket, he would select two packets of frozen food (which in the 1950s was far removed from what your supermarket offers you today), pop them in the oven and proudly present you with unpalatable meat, potatoes and gravy. He once took me to tea at his club, the Athenaeum. Given the bill, he fished in his jacket pocket for an envelope (which I presumed contained his allotted spending money for the day) and extracted from it the necessary cash (£1, as I recall).

Cadbury's thriftiness was well known to the staff. Geoffrey Goodman, probably the most discerning industrial writer of our time, still remembers an occasion when he led a union team to negotiate a wage claim with the chairman. In Goodman's words:

We were called into that inelegant room of his on the top floor to find him sitting back in his chair stretching out his red braces. I started to read out our pay claim and referred to the fact that the *News Chronicle* at that time was paying its reporters and sub-editors, on average, less than any national paper except the Communist *Daily Worker* [as it was then called]. Cadbury pushed back his chair, lifted his hands into the air and roared with laughter (one of the few times I ever saw him laugh). 'Lower than any paper apart from the *Daily Worker*,' he repeated, mixing words and laughter. 'Splendid – at last I can say a good word for the jolly old *Worker*.' We did not get our pay rise.

Tom Baistow, who was foreign editor in my time and is today one of the shrewdest critics of the newspaper scene, recalled for me two examples of the Cadbury attitude to money. Here they are, in Tom's own words:

One lunchtime in the fifties I found myself walking up Bouverie Street from the *News Chronicle* with the proprietor, Laurence Cadbury. 'Where do you lunch, Tom?' he asked.

I told him I was heading for the Wellington, a restaurant just round the corner in Fleet Street, where friends like Michael Foot, James Cameron and Paul Johnson met for a meal.

'How much does lunch there cost?' was his next question.

'Between about five shillings and seven and sixpence – the proprietress is Belgian and the food is very good.'

Cadbury gave one of his famous giggles: 'Much more than I pay! I'm going to the Bank of England' (he was then a director of the Bank) 'where there's what you might call a subsidised canteen' (another giggle) 'that serves a very good lunch for one-and-nine!'

When we reached the top of the street he remarked: 'I wonder why I have to walk to the other side of the railway bridge at Ludgate to get to the Bank for tuppence-ha'penny, yet on the way back I catch the same bus outside the Bank and it takes me to Bouverie Street for the same fare. Perhaps you people should do a leader-page article about the anomalies of London Transport.' With a cheery wave he set off for Ludgate Circus.

On another occasion, when I was foreign editor, he came into my room and asked me if the peseta exchange rate was favourable from the sterling point of view. 'Joyce' (his wife) 'rather fancies going to Spain and I wondered how much it would cost.' I explained that there was a special tourist rate that offered a discount of almost 50 per cent. 'That sounds very interesting indeed,' he commented.

'You'll find Spain interesting despite Franco,' I replied, having been there the year before.

Later that summer he strolled into my office sporting a very deep tan. 'You obviously enjoyed Spain,' I said.

'We didn't go to Spain after all' (giggle) 'we went to Greece instead. I discovered that you get a lot more drachmae for your pound.'

On the subject of meanness (more of disposition than of money), Tom has another cautionary recollection of his *News Chronicle* days. Here it is:

It was lunchtime, a summer's day in 1957, the place El Vino, Fleet Street's favourite watering hole when there was a Fleet Street. Round the counter gate at the entrance a bunch of us were exchanging the gossip of the day: James Cameron and myself, from the *News Chronicle*, Vicky the cartoonist, Hugh Cudlipp, Bill (Cassandra) Connor, Sydney Jacobson, all from the *Mirror*, and a few others. The manager then was Frank Bower, who affected Edwardian 'gentleman's' wear, embroidered 'weskits' and a curly-brimmed bowler, and he had laid down stuffy rules about customers' dress – no tie, no drink – and no women to be served at the bar – a ruling that was to produce a lot of hilarious copy when feminists later took the Vino to court.

Spotting Frank's baroque bowler behind the counter partition, I reached round for it on impulse and stuck it on Vicky's head. As it fell down to his ears, he spread his hands wide in a caricature of a Jewish dealer and said: 'Anyvun got any old clothes they vant to sell?'

At that moment Frank appeared from the other end of the bar, saw his beloved bowler on an alien head and roared: 'How dare you take such a disgraceful liberty! Hand that hat back at once. If anything like this ever happens again I shall not permit you to frequent this establishment.' Immediately I explained that it was my rather childish idea of a joke. 'Never try such a trick again or I will ban you too,' he declared imperiously.

'If that's how you treat a harmless bit of fun I don't know whether I'd want to use your *pub*,' I replied, knowing the word would wound.

'I for one won't be using it again, you pompous old publican,' said Hugh Cudlipp. Turning to us, he added: 'Let's find a more congenial place where the landlord's hat isn't as tight as this fellow's.' And we walked out. Not just because Bower had been so pompous but because we suspected that he wouldn't have created such a fuss if I had put his bowler on an Aryan head.

With typical Cudlippian panache, Hugh celebrated our act of self-abnegation by throwing a splendid lunch at the Café Royal at which we were each provided with a curly bowler that was ceremoniously punched through the crown when the brandy was served. Typically, also, Cudlipp was the only member of the group who never again set foot in El Vino. He now, of course, has the freedom of the bar in the House of Lords.

If Cadbury was not the enemy, he was hardly a staunch ally in the battle Michael Curtis waged to save the *News Chronicle*. Even before he became editor, Michael had proposed to the board that money be invested in taking the paper out of the popular rat-race and directing its radical appeal to the post-war generation of young people who wanted an intelligent, unbigoted newspaper presented in an easily readable format. Wrongly concluding that he had been promoted to the editorship because the board approved his ideas, he developed them in greater detail and, early in 1954, suggested to the management that the paper be turned from a broadsheet into a serious tabloid, arguing that it should not only be different but should also look different. Cadbury, who perhaps had never seen *Le Monde*, had the *idée fixe* that the only definition of a tabloid was the brash *Daily Mirror*. The idea was dropped and never mentioned again until after the *News Chronicle*'s death.

Michael's next move was to create an opportunity, in discussion with Sydney Bernstein, for the *News Chronicle* to take a stake in Granada Television. That was in the days before Granada became, in the words of Lord Thomson describing his ownership of another television network, 'a licence to print money'. Once again the giggling Cadbury turned down an idea which could have made the paper solvent. It must have been desperation that drove Michael to his next proposition – that the *News Chronicle* should merge with the ailing *Daily Herald*, the combined production being a Lib–Lab paper but independent of either party. Given the quality of the two managements, that could have been a disastrous venture but by then Michael was probably convinced that Cadbury's main concern was how to get rid of the sick man of Fleet Street and compensate the staff for whom no proper pension scheme had been devised.

By the time I joined the paper a breathing space had been provided by Lord Layton, a former chairman but then in semi-retirement as vice-chairman. He engineered the merger of the *Chronicle* with the *Daily Dispatch*, a Tory-inclined paper published in Manchester. It was a technical success which immediately raised the daily sales above the danger point, but it was to be short lived. My first task was to take over the features department. Now I numbered among my colleagues the matchless James Cameron, whose sculptured sentences were a joy equalled only by his intimate knowledge and descriptions of the best bars in every country of the world; Ian Trethowan, the shrewd observer of the political scene who was to become director general of the BBC; Bruce Rothwell, the probing Washington correspondent, who, at the time of his sudden death from a heart attack in 1984, was Rupert Murdoch's right-hand man; Boris Kidel, the *bon viveur* who reported with verve from Paris; Leslie Mallory, the wittiest of show business writers; and Sylvain Mangeot, the wise foreign editor who habitually fell asleep in the middle of a conference, not from boredom but from an obscure ailment.

I was, alas, too late to meet the brilliant Ian Mackay who fell dead on Morecambe promenade at the end of the Labour Party

Conference of 1952, but his memory was fresh in the office and I am, again, indebted to Geoffrey Goodman for this story about that peerless writer:

When he was the *News Chronicle*'s industrial correspondent and before he started to write that magnificent regular column, Ian used to go the rounds of the trades union conferences and, like so many of us, he occasionally landed back in his hotel room somewhat the worse for the sauce. At one seaside watering hole Ian, back in his room, badly needing to pee but, too far gone to find his way out of his room to the loo, used the wash basin, being a man of enterprise. However he was a big chap and he fell on the basin. The whole fitting then came away from the wall, the pipes burst and water cascaded over Ian as he was peeing and generally laid waste the splendid bedroom. Ian's first reaction was to phone the office and ask the switchboard what time it was.

There was never a staff so devoted to a newspaper as the journalists on the *News Chronicle* (even though, being a troop of true radicals, they all held divergent views about what we should be doing); and there was never a staff so betrayed. I had not long been a member of the doomed team when, in October 1956, Anthony Eden plunged us into the murky waters of Suez. There was never any doubt about where we stood – with one outstanding exception, Laurence Cadbury, who admired Eden and was a firm supporter of his policy. All credit to him, then, that he allowed Michael Curtis to exercise the traditional right of the editor to decide the policy of the paper and to fight Eden to the bitter end. In retrospect, it is possible to forgive Cadbury for his one peccadillo. At the height of the crisis, and aghast at a swingeing attack on the government by James Cameron, he secretly telephoned our Manchester editor, whose sympathies also lay with Eden, and arranged for certain vital paragraphs in Cameron's article to be 'lost in transition' from London to Manchester and thereby deleted from our northern editions.

When the guns fell silent I was entrusted by Michael with the welcome though challenging labour of reconstructing the whole, sorry affair. I drew up a list of searching questions which were circulated to eight of our foremost correspondents in London, Paris, Washington and Tel Aviv. Entirely due to their expert, diligent and penetrating probes behind the scenes, I was able to collate and edit enough material to present, in the second week of December, a four-part series which, if immodesty may be forgiven, has stood the test of time.

In a more light-hearted moment I published, at Bruce Rothwell's suggestion, the verbatim text of an Eisenhower Press conference. With its string of rambling, inarticulate, unfinished sentences and its meaningless mumbo jumbo, it became known in the office as the piece that passeth all understanding.

In 1956 I made my first appearance on television as one of the judges in the *Chronicle*'s 'Be Your Own Boss' competition, which would have delighted Margaret Thatcher because it was designed to encourage bright young people with ambitions to start their own businesses. The winner received enough prize money to provide the initial capital. After the competition – one of the first Fleet Street wheezes to be taken up by television – had been running for some time we thought it would be a good idea to check back on an early winner, see how his business was faring and write a story about him. Unfortunately the one we chose had blued all his prize money on wine, women and song. Charles Widdup, an unflappable, stalwart member of the night production team, recalls a similar mishap: 'The *Chronicle*, bless its liberal heart, once ran an essay competition on the theme of world peace. The distinguished judges awarded the prize to a woman who wrote from an address that suggested a fine country house. James Cameron was dispatched to interview her and found the poor soul was a patient in a mental hospital.'

Bill Hicks, the eminent sports editor, has a tale with a happier ending:

A little after three o'clock one April afternoon I was handed a telegram, the like of which I doubt has been received by any sports editor before or since. It came from Brixton prison and was sent by a specialist contributor, not a member of staff but well known in his sporting field. It read: 'AM IN BRIXTON FOR £38 DEBT. CAN YOU HELP?' We rang the prison. They said that if we delivered the £38 in cash by five o'clock we could have our man. The money was immediately found and a taxi was called. With three minutes to spare our debtor journalist came joyfully from his cell and, an hour later, was sitting in the office writing a sports story.

Not long after the Suez series was published I was asked to visit the 'glass house', that black architectural horror which was the home of the *Daily Express*. Harold Keeble told me that Lord Beaverbrook, foreseeing the demise of the *News Chronicle*, wanted to take on some of the staff. Would I join the *Express*? I could only reply that I would not be the first rat to leave the sinking ship but, if the Beaver would wait upon events, I would join if and when the ship went down. At our next meeting Keeble told me that the Beaver would brook no delay. I would either join now or not at all. The answer was not at all.

For the *News Chronicle* the aftermath of Suez was the beginning of the end. When the smoke cleared, we had lost some 40,000 sales, mainly desertions by the newly acquired readers of the *Daily Dispatch*. The vast majority of our longstanding readers stood stolidly behind us. We were now in the shadow of death. We had to move fast to delay, if not defy, mortality. What was done, and what was left undone, are best told in the words of Michael Curtis, in a letter he wrote to the *New Statesman* in November 1964:

Between us [Michael and Mike] we worked out the kind of paper we wanted and produced dummies [examples] to show the board what it would look like. These dummies, incidentally, were broadsheet and *not* tabloid in size. I proposed that we should take the extreme step of increasing the price to 3*d* at a time when our competitors (including the *Telegraph*) were selling at $2\frac{1}{2}d$. The extra revenue – amounting to about £20,000 a day even if the circulation went down by 25 per cent to the million mark – would have been shared between the cost of extra newsprint for a larger paper, additional editorial staff, a properly planned publicity campaign, and ... a sinking fund for the staff if the gamble failed.

With this plan we should have had £$\frac{1}{2}$ million extra revenue for the next twelve months, since I believed our advertisers would continue to support the paper for this period. We also had the advantage of a fanatically loyal readership who, if the situation had been properly explained to them, would also have supported us. On this basis I calculated that for twelve months we could not be worse off and might conceivably turn the corner.

With this last-ditch plan I proceeded to pester the board of directors, the trustees and various members of the Cadbury family ... In the end all this activity came to nothing. I had no alternative but to offer my resignation (accepted no doubt with considerable relief) knowing in my own mind that the *News Chronicle* could now only drift into oblivion.

So Michael departed and became, for the next thirty years, a valuable and trusted aide to the Aga Khan. I was asked to step into his shoes. Summoned to Cadbury's office, I found him flanked by his two top management men, Messrs Coope and Crosland (the three C's, we called them). I asked if we could agree on a policy for the paper. Cadbury giggled and said: 'You edit the paper for three months and then we'll discuss policy.' As an afterthought, he produced a copy of that day's *Daily Mail* and asked why the *News Chronicle* could not be like that. I explained why not, left his office and tendered my resignation.

How little grasp poor Cadbury had on detail is best demonstrated by quoting, again from the *New Statesman*, what he wrote in two letters to that publication in October 1964. In the first he pointed out that 'the editor of the merged *Daily Mail* and *News Chronicle* [by then myself] was at one time editor of the latter paper'. To which I replied that I was never editor of the *News Chronicle*. In his next letter Cadbury wrote: 'In reply to Mr Randall he is technically right. After the resignation of Mr Curtis he continued to edit the paper, but without the official title, until the termination of his contract. The point at issue between both gentlemen and the board was that the latter were not prepared to turn the paper into a tabloid.'

I had perforce to write one more letter. It said: 'Briefly, and I hope for the last time, to correct Mr Laurence Cadbury: I *never* edited the *News Chronicle* – with or without the title. I was an assistant editor and so remained in the short time between the resignation of Michael Curtis and my departure ... Throughout my time on the *News Chronicle* the question of turning it into a tabloid never arose.'

What did arise, when Fleet Street heard of my resignation, was an approach from three sources – Denis Hamilton at Kemsley House (from which I had been banned in 1953), the *Daily Herald* and the *Daily Mail*. The *Mail* won because William Hardcastle, the deputy editor, invited me to meet him at the American bar in the Savoy Hotel where, over the sixth dry martini (his were on the rocks), we clinched a deal with, as far as I was concerned, a distinctly trembling handshake. I was to be at the *Mail* when, on a mournful day, the *News Chronicle*, in great secrecy and without the knowledge of its loyal staff, was delivered into our hands.

In a last desperate bid to keep the title alive, a *News Chronicle* action committee of four, which included Arthur Butler, a sharp-witted member of the political team, went to plead with Roy Thomson to buy the paper and keep its identity alive. Thomson congratulated 'you young men' on their loyalty. 'I admire your spirit,' he said, 'but I am not a philanthropist.' He later bought *The Times* and poured millions into it.

6

Christmas Is Coming

It was not so much that I was now a fish out of water, more a dog which had lost its bark. However long you have been in journalism (a trade in which some will master, and others will maul, the English language), transition from one office to another is never a smooth crossing. Some writers who have previously been nursed and nurtured begin to wilt when they are transplanted and left to fend for themselves; the same applies to executives. Two newspapers may have similar aims but use quite different methods to achieve them. The new arrival has to get the feel of the paper and weigh up the key personalities, divining where modesty cloaks great skill or lack of competence hides behind aggression. This was not made easy for me by Arthur Wareham, the *Daily Mail* editor in 1957, whose identikit might resemble that of a bishop but who appeared, despite his quiet, friendly, almost self-effacing manner, to be quite content for the paper to pay out many thousands of pounds a year in settling lawsuits brought against his gossip column which sometimes descended into the sewage of life.

Apart from giving me my first company car (long remembered are the joys of free motoring with tax, insurance, petrol, servicing and repairs all paid for), Wareham made me executive editor with very little to execute. Nominally I had a roving commission overseeing the features and pictures departments but, since each of them was run by a perfectly competent section head who resented being put under my authority, I had to tread the hazardous path between stepping into friction and retreating to my glass-walled office, trying to look as if I was working against the clock on a (non-existent) article. To find yourself idle in a newspaper office is like climbing into bed with Marilyn Monroe and falling fast asleep – unless the idleness is caused by that terrifying phenomenon, the word blockage. There were some exceptions to the general rule – a few journalists who perfected the art of doing nothing. Ian Jack once shared a corner of the *Sunday Times Magazine* with, as he recounts,

a distinguished writer of remarkably low productivity. One morning around eleven he came in and said: 'It's a nightmare. I have to phone Lord Clark.' Nothing happened. His hand did not reach for the telephone. He smoked a few cigarettes, talked to his friends and, at one o'clock, went out to lunch, returning at 3.30. 'It's a nightmare,' he said. 'I really must phone Lord Clark.' This time his fingers did make contact with the phone and he began to dial the long code for the lord's country house but after the first three numbers he gave up. 'What a nightmare . . .' He went home around five. Another hard day at the office.

My monotonous inactivity continued for many a boring month, relieved only by a visit to Kenya. Michael Curtis, former editor of the *News Chronicle*, had founded for the Aga Khan the East African Newspaper Group, based in Nairobi. He invited me, all expenses paid (including a first-class flight on the 'Whispering Giant', as the Britannia aircraft was then known, and a stopover in Paris on the way home), to stay with him, explore the political scene and decide if I would like to join him. Fascinated as I was by the black vanguard and the white rearguard in Kenya and by the opportunity to use the new newspaper technology almost thirty years before Wapping, I declined Michael's offer in the belief that chance, my constant companion, would lift me out of the rut into which I had fallen at the *Mail*. When I returned to the office and wrote a 6,000-word report on Kenya which nobody bothered to read, I felt I had made the wrong decision.

But Christmas 1959 was coming and, as so often in the *Mail*'s history, it brought no cheer to the editor. Late in December Arthur Wareham was summoned, at short notice, to Warwick House, Lord Rothermere's elegant London home in a backwater near the Mall. Wareham told a few of his colleagues that he was sure his proprietor was going to congratulate him on his year's work and reward him with a generous increase in salary. On his return he called the entire staff into his office and announced that he had been fired and would be clearing out his desk that night before handing us over to his successor, William Hardcastle. That is the way of the newspaper world.

Under Hardcastle I was put in charge of the paper at night, starting at four in the afternoon and finishing somewhere between one and three in the morning, depending on the night's events. It was an exciting, demanding, but often frustrating labour. A night editor has little say in the major content of the paper. By the time you take over, the day staff have almost completed the feature pages and decided what news stories should have the greatest coverage and what picture assignments should be given to the best photographers. The night editor's first task is to assimilate the long schedules produced by the home news, foreign, picture and sports editors, detailing who is doing what and indicating the potential strength of the stories and when the copy may be ready. You then check progress with the departmental heads and have a quick discussion with your staff before going into the evening conference, where the editor makes the important decisions while you often wish you had been in at the conception rather than being left to deliver the child. All you can do is take the material you have been given, improve it, project it to the best of your ability and make sure it goes to press on time. Should a major story break during the night you will then be put on your editing mettle and given the chance, if you handle it better than your rivals, to derive one of the greatest satisfactions a journalist can have.

Hardcastle was the fastest reactor to news I have ever worked with – and the list includes Charles Wilson, now editor of *The Times*, who runs him a close second. Given what is called a 'flash' (the first indication on the news agency tapes that a big story is breaking), Hardcastle would decide, by the time he had smoked half a Chesterfield cigarette, which reporters and photographers should be sent where, how they should be briefed, what background material should be prepared, what feature page should be cleared to accommodate it, and which experts should be contacted for their opinions. Despite that adeptness, Hardcastle had, from a night editor's viewpoint, a disturbing weakness: he greatly admired, and sometimes slavishly aped, our main rival, the *Daily Express*, at a time when I felt that paper had passed its peak and was heading into decline.

There was an unofficial arrangement in Fleet Street whereby night editors received the first editions of their main competitors soon after they came off the presses. In offices where there was a lack of confidence (which there was in the *Mail* in 1960, partly due to the fact that most of the management regarded the *Express* as a far better paper, and partly due to the sales figures, which showed that the *Express* was still heavily outselling us) the arrival of the other papers could lead to absurdities and aberrations. No matter if the *Mail* had good stories that the *Express* had not covered, if the *Express* had an 'exclusive' the night staff were obliged to chase the story and produce a version of it in the last edition. It was a pernicious custom which I tried in vain to break.

Hardcastle would leave the office at 6 p.m. to relax with his cronies and his dry martinis, pop back at 8 p.m. for a quick check with me on how things were shaping, and then go home. He would ring me when he knew I had received the first edition of the *Express*. I would tell him how the *Mail* looked, what the main stories were and what changes we were making in later editions. Then would come the inevitable question: 'What's in the *Express*?' One night I told him that in the last column of the *Express* front page there was a story which we had checked out and found to be false and therefore I was not going to print a word of it.

Hardcastle ordered me to read him the *Express* story in full. When I had finished, he said: 'That's a bloody good story, Mike, run it.'

I protested: 'But it's all balls, Bill. I assure you we have gone into it in detail and it simply does not stand up. I wouldn't touch it with a bargepole.'

That made no impression on Hardcastle. 'Look, Mike,' he said, 'I know a good story when I see one and I am telling you to get that one into the *Mail* tonight.' And he hung up. The small version that was eventually printed in the *Mail* bore little resemblance to the original *Express* story, and neither of us mentioned the incident next day.

Hardcastle understood the frustrations felt by a night editor who could take no part in the creation of the paper and, by way of compensation, started to involve me in the political lunches he gave in a private room at the Stafford Hotel, off St James's Street. It was there that I had the first of many encounters with Harold Wilson – and my only meeting with George Brown. It must have been in the run-up to the General Election of 1961 because I recall telling Brown that I was dismayed by the unimpressive Labour Party posters. 'I don't know who dreams them up,' I said, 'but any journalist who can write good head-lines could do twenty times better.'

Brown flared up and demanded: 'Which university did you go to?' I told him that I had been turned down by Oxford and had not applied elsewhere. 'In that case,' he bellowed in a voice that could be heard far beyond the dining room, 'you are not fit to hold your bloody job.' At the other end of the table Wilson's face clearly reflected his discomfort. I refilled Brown's glass and quickly changed the subject.

Years later I was consulted by Wilson's henchwoman, Marcia Williams (now Lady Falkender), about what the public reaction would be if Brown were eased out of the Foreign Office. By that time Brown's 'tired and emotional' (a *Private Eye* euphemism) scenes had unfortunately become so frequent and embarrassing that I reluctantly said that I thought the majority of people would consider him no longer fitted to be Foreign Secretary and therefore his departure was not likely to damage Wilson's government. I have known some good ministerial drinkers (Harold Macmillan and Wilson among them) and I feel some sympathy with the character in Ian Jack's book, *Before the Oil Ran Out*, who said that Margaret Thatcher would be all the better for a few large ones. Alas, George Brown was all the worse for too many large ones.

By the time I joined the *Mail* I had completed the political cycle, from the voice of high Toryism at Kemsley House, via the Labour megaphone of the *Daily Mirror* and the Liberal cadences of the *News Chronicle*, to the Conservative trumpeting of the *Daily Mail*. If journalists worked only for the paper whose political views coincided with theirs, most of them, since they are either apolitical or lean to the Left, would be out of work. They do not enter the profession to become political propagandists; the majority derive the greatest satisfaction from being encouraged to go out and gather the facts with which they can impart, as fully and accurately as possible, the information on which judgements can be made. Some, of course, are corrupted by orders to slant their stories in a particular direction (witness Neil Kinnock's visit to America shortly before the 1987 General Election when some of the hounds were scenting disaster before the hunt for the facts had even begun); others, who work for the tabloid Press, have to compromise with the limitations imposed by the severely restricted space they are allotted. Most of them, in my experience, are happiest in the pursuit of truth; few of them give more than a cursory glance to the predictable leading articles in their papers, knowing that they could write them in their sleep.

Is it not an insult to the public, who are politically more astute than newspaper proprietors or editors realise, that a paper should instruct its readers to vote one way or another in a General Election? Fortunately, the Press does not sway elections and governments are not chosen by leader writers who, though they may profess to present balanced arguments, at the final count only echo their masters' voices, be they Rupert Murdoch and Lord Rothermere on the Right, or Robert Maxwell on the Left. It is not true that the compelling 'Vote for Him' (the returning soldier) campaign in the *Daily Mirror* was responsible for Clement Attlee's victory in 1945 any more than the Tory Press brought about the Labour débâcle in 1983. As for 1987, most media pundits proclaimed the victor of the election campaign to be Neil Kinnock, with that sleek, slick, schooled, presidential-like presentation of a one-man band that was playing the people's favourite tune. The electorate clearly thought otherwise. As Cecil King, the former chairman of the *Mirror* group, said in the 1950s, 'The Press can only kick at an open door,' words he must have forgotten when he later plotted to unseat Harold Wilson and was, as a result, booted out of office.

Lord Beaverbook was honest enough to tell a Royal Commission on the Press that he ran newspapers 'for the propaganda, of course, so I can have my say, persuade people. Not to make money.' His powers of persuasion were so slight that he probably lost more causes (including the Empire) than any other proprietor. The sermonising leading article is part of the automatic-reaction school of journalism which has long bedevilled Fleet Street – 'We stand for this therefore we will attack that.' No need to give the subject any deeper thought, which is convenient because, within the confines of the average leading article, there is not much room for thought. All praise, then, to the *Independent* which, in 1987, did not advocate voting for any one party, but left its readers to decide for themselves.

Had I been asked about my political stance before I joined the *Mail*, I would have replied that I voted Tory in 1945, out of a sentimental wish to thank Winston Churchill for his blood, sweat, toil and tears, and that I had voted Labour ever since (as I continued to do until 1987 when I found myself so at odds with all parties that I could not force my steps to the polling booth). But I was not asked about my policies because William Hardcastle, himself no Tory, would have regarded the question as irrelevant.

In the course of 1961 Hardcastle decided that he wanted me to become his deputy editor, a post that had not been filled since Wareham's departure. This brought me my third new company car in four years. The car as a status symbol on the *Mail* had by now reached such preposterous proportions that it became more important to some executives than their titles or their salaries. I had begun, happily enough, with a Ford Consul. But within two years I was ordered to exchange it for something superior, the reason being that Donald Todhunter had been hired from the *Express* as news editor. The *Mail*'s way of luring him on to the staff included the promise of a better car than the *Express* had allotted him. But I was senior to him and, by *Mail* management decree, Todhunter could not have a more expensive car than mine, so my Consul was replaced by a Wolseley 6/90 which, when I became deputy editor, was in turn superseded by a costly Citroën. We filled our petrol tanks at a garage where the company had an account and where, on a Friday, we would pump in enough gallons to keep us going over the weekend.

Hardcastle had only just begun the painful process of trying to liberalise the *Mail* when it suddenly absorbed the *News Chronicle*. It was a marriage of unequals and the wedding was conducted in a manner that could only offend the loyal body of *Chronicle* readers who, without warning, received one morning the combined paper. It was not to their taste and they soon turned to other papers for their daily diet of news, rapidly reducing the *Mail*'s falsely boosted circulation. I have never understood why it was thought necessary to carry out the merger in such secrecy that some members of the *News Chronicle* staff were encouraged, the day before, to prepare the early feature page for the next night's issue which the management knew would never be printed, while others learned of the murder of their paper only by watching TV news. Laurence Cadbury's defence was that, but for the clandestine operation, he would not have received the £2 million (a paltry sum even then) which he needed to compensate his staff (in a small way). I can only assume that Lord Rothermere, or his senior management, made secrecy a condition of the deal in the mistaken belief that, if overnight you put the merged paper through letter-boxes and on to bookstalls as a *fait accompli*, *News Chronicle* readers would have to accept it. They did not and Hardcastle's lot became the harder for their desertion. There is nothing so depressing as the downward curve on a circulation chart.

Some members of the *News Chronicle* staff joined the *Mail*, among them James Cameron, who, soon after his arrival, was the subject of a special conference. The problem was to find some country in the world which this far-flung correspondent (who had already been flung further than most of his contemporaries) had not yet visited. Poring over maps, we hopefully pointed our fingers at various remote lands, only to find that Cameron had once, if not twice, covered the territory. Finally, someone asked if he had ever been to Blackpool. He had not and, since a Labour Party Conference was assembling there, he was on the next train. The result was vintage Cameronese:

To be exposed abruptly and cruelly to the impact of Blackpool itself is not a thing one recovers from within twenty-four hours, and a richer therapy is needed even than the dulcet companionship of Mr Ian Mikardo at a Victory for Socialism brains trust.

This is incomparably the most hideous centre of human habitation I have ever seen in a rich and varied life, not excepting Mukden in Manchuria, which until this day I had held to be the rockbottom of urban man's achievement.

Add to this an hotel, built in the early Auschwitz manner, which is as primitive an establishment as ever I hope to experience again, and you have a situation that even a warm smile from the leader would not readily soften.

There may well be more charmless neighbourhoods, perhaps on the far side of the moon, but Blackpool front will do me for the time being.

As deputy editor I increasingly wanted to have some influence over the general direction of the paper. I did not agree with the assumption that we needed a juicy divorce case as the main page-three story, or a sordid tale of crime as the major attraction on page five; nor did I see why the gossip writer should continually pry, with a leer and a smear, into people's private lives. At one time the *Mail*'s 'Tanfield' column was run by a man who would arrive in the office and announce to his staff: 'Today I'm going to crucify so-and-so. Can't stand the man.' I also wanted to make better use of the space devoted to the cavortings of coupling (or un-coupling) partners whose names were held to be newsworthy although they were often nonentities. Across the lunchtable, from the dry martinis to the brandy, I put these thoughts to Hardcastle and tried to persuade him that the way forward lay in lifting the *Mail* out of the rut of trivia, and in breaking the popular paper mould by replacing much of what I called the 'off-the-peg' news with material that was largely of our own creation. Our reporting, I believed, should have a deeper, more enquiring approach; it should not accept things at face value, or react automatically to events, but should discover the whys and wherefores and give our readers the fullest possible information, backed up with expert interpretation by our specialists in every field from politics to sport. I outlined (shades of Curtis and the *Chronicle*) a quality/popular paper with a respect for the individual, a reverence for accuracy, a sense of humour, a widening range of interests and a rising standard of writing.

Hardcastle, burdened by a falling circulation, recoiled from the idea of changing course, with all the risks he believed it entailed. I did not then know that his relations with Lord Rothermere and the senior management were becoming increasingly strained. Soon after that lunch, late in 1962, the office was abuzz with rumours (as all newspaper offices constantly are) that Hardcastle was going the way of all expendable editors (he was the sixth post-war occupant of the chair). Since Christmas was coming I took the rumours seriously and confronted the managing director, Bobby Redhead, demanding to know the truth. He refused to deny or confirm, which, as all students of political statements will know, is tantamount to confirmation. I told Redhead that if Hardcastle went (and I saw no valid reason why he should) it would be fatal for the *Mail* if an outsider were imported from another paper as the next editor. I was not, I explained, applying for the job myself although naturally, as the deputy, I was bound to be a candidate, but I was pleading for the continuity that could only be achieved if the new editor was promoted from among the paper's present senior staff.

The next day I was commanded to journey to Daylesford, Rothermere's Cotswold home, where the proprietor questioned me closely on where I thought the *Mail*'s future lay. I put to him the plan I had already suggested to Hardcastle. When I had finished, Rothermere explained that he was worried about Hardcastle's health and was sending him on a trip round the world. He would like me to be acting editor of the paper in Hardcastle's absence. I enquired how long that would be. 'Wait and see,' said Rothermere. Hardcastle left the office to start his travels just before Christmas. He never returned. After three months of caretaking I was appointed editor in April 1963. 'You have chosen the hardest course,' said Rothermere, 'and good luck to you.'

7

In the Chair

Where the buck stopped, there sat I, in a state of bewilderment, bordering on fear, at having attained, at forty-three, one of the most coveted positions in Fleet Street. There were, in 1963, only nine national daily newspapers and therefore, though my maths have always been suspect, only eight other men in the country holding a similar post. (Could it be that the proprietors' penchant, in those days, for booting editors out of their chairs at frequent intervals sprang from a benevolent desire to share these rarefied jobs among as many people as possible?) Any elation I might have felt was soon dispelled as I discovered what Rothermere meant by the 'hardest course', though he did his best to smooth it by providing me with a magnificent Mercedes, driven by John, a uniformed chauffeur of great skill and deep discretion. Rothermere also moved me into an elegant office which he had just vacated and from which I soon removed, at a bargain price negotiated with His Lordship, the steel coal scuttle and fire-irons which, since the office fireplace had been blocked up, served a better purpose in the hearth of my Richmond home.

Now that actions had to speak louder than words, I suffered an immediate loss of confidence which was not ameliorated by a series of unwelcome surprises. The first came when I sent for statistical details of the *Mail*'s readership and learned, to my dismay, that every year at least 70,000 of my readers would die. Whereas 16 per cent of the British population was over sixty-five, 21 per cent of our customers were in that age group, which meant that I had to gain 70,000 readers annually just to stand still. It was no comfort to me to be told that 3,000 of our faithful readers were members of the clergy and 9,000 were publicans, much as I needed the ministrations of both professions.

The second surprise was an instrument of torment that stood on a table behind my desk. It was an intercom machine which, in my innocence, I first regarded as a great asset since it afforded me, at the flick of a switch, instant contact with any of the departmental heads. But the instrument had another, and rather sinister, function: it gave senior management immediate access to me. When they buzzed they caused a coloured light to appear, which not only identified the caller but also demanded that, whatever I was doing, I must depress the relevant switch and receive their call which came loud and clear through a microphone.

The most frequent user of this machine was the vice-chairman, the then Hon. Vere (or 'Mere Vere' as *Private Eye* dubbed him) Harmsworth, son of the proprietor and now Lord Rothermere, a highly successful owner and a man of considerable charm. His opening remark was always the same: 'Did you see that marvellous story about such-and-such in the *Express* this morning? Why wasn't it in the *Mail*?' I might be holding a conference with senior staff but I would have to break off and explain to the Hon. Vere, for the umpteenth time, that my policy was to produce a paper markedly different from the *Express* and that was why I had ignored his favourite story which I regarded as a non-story. I would then point out to him the stories that had appeared in the *Mail* that morning and could not be found in the *Express*. To my embarrassment, because my executives could hear every word of both sides of the conversation, he would wave aside my arguments and persist in his praise for the *Express*. He had, of course, every right to expound his sincerely held views but I felt they were misguided.

Most of the top management appeared to be *Express* fans, with the honourable exceptions of Marmaduke Hussey, now chairman of the BBC Board of Governors, and Bob Hammond, the new managing director, who, apart from being an understanding employer and a generous host, derived the greatest pleasure from television by watching it with the sound turned off (try it next time you view Sir Robin Day's 'Question Time' and if it does not give you a laugh a minute I fear for your sense of humour).

When Hammond's light glowed on the intercom he would question me closely about why I had given such prominence, or short shrift, to a particular story. This usually meant he was having trouble defending my decisions to fellow directors (only one of whom had been a journalist). Appreciating his motives, I would go along to his office and attempt to sharpen his sword by giving him a detailed explanation of my actions. We built up a great respect for each other and, in the end, my downfall was also his.

Perhaps the grossest misuse of the infernal machine was made by the advertising director, who came on the air to upbraid me for running a perfectly valid front-page item on a cost-cutting exercise by Marks and Spencer. His bitter complaint was that I had given free publicity to a firm which did not buy advertising space from us. There was only one answer to such a ludicrously narrow-minded, if not immoral, argument and that was to cut it off by an angry flick of the switch. Although management could have no product without journalists, many of them regarded us as little better than a necessary nuisance.

The third surprise was to discover that Lord Rothermere did not often have the spine, spunk, spark or spirit to back his editor when it most mattered. In addition to my obligatory phone call on his direct line every evening at 5.30 (two minutes either side were not appreciated) to discuss the day's news and persuade him that we were taking a sensible (though not necessarily totally Tory) stance in the leading article, I had to dine about twice a month at his London home. The routine was always the same. On my arrival the flunkey would pour a large dry martini. That consumed, we would go into dinner and

Rothermere would indulge his liking for political gossip, the more scurrilous the better. Only over the brandy could I steer the conversation to the *Daily Mail* and seek his approval for my next innovations. Having finally got what I wanted – a terse 'Yes, good idea. You do that,' – I would confidently, on my return to the office, put plans into action, only to be reprimanded a few days later on the 5.30 telephone call.

'What in hell do you think you're doing?' he would ask. 'Why have you let the *Daily Mail* say that?' In vain I would remind him that we had agreed it over dinner. 'We agreed nothing of the sort. I don't remember anything of that nature. Certainly not. You must have completely misunderstood me,' he would snap.

I would know what had happened. One of his influential friends, or some high Tory, had been attacking him for what had appeared in the *Mail* and he was too weak to support me. Sometimes, on those calls, I could hear voices in the background and assumed that he was trying to impress his guests. He would not do as Lord Thomson did, replying to criticism of his papers by saying: 'Why don't you take it up with my editor? He has his freedom.'

The fourth surprise was the number of decisions that had to be taken in any one day. I once kept a check and my score was 200. They might range from the selection of the main front-page story to the resolution of a reporter's financial problems but they all had to be made by the editor. On the *News Chronicle* Michael Curtis maintained that if 50 per cent of his daily decisions, most of them taken against the clock, proved to be right, he had done well. He reckoned that any editor who scored higher than that was either a genius or uncommonly lucky. Richard Crossman once told me he thought being an editor was harder than being a cabinet minister but easier than being a prime minister. I did not demur.

My day began at 7 a.m. when every morning paper landed on my bed and, with the aid of tea and tobacco, I combed them, beginning with the last edition of the *Mail* which I would not have seen the night before. It was essential to assess, before I reached the office, how we compared with our rivals, which topics must be reflected in that day's feature articles, which stories were only half told and needed further delving and which subjects the leading article might tackle. If you are in the business there is a technique for the swift reading of newspapers. You instinctively know what you can safely skip and what requires your attention. Since I was driven to the office I could leave the last of my reading (which might include an article I had brought home the night before) to be done in the back of the car, where I would also scribble notes to myself all over the white spaces in *The Times*.

Once in the office there was no time for reading. Some problem would always await me. It might be the foreign editor wanting approval to overspend his budget by dispatching a correspondent to cover the latest African crisis; it might be the advertisement manager seeking to put his case for exceeding his quota of advertising columns and robbing me of editorial space; or it might be a complaint that required instant response.

One morning I arrived at the office to find on my desk a message that an irate Roy Thomson (then owner of the *Sunday Times* and other former Kemsley newspapers) had been on the phone demanding that I call him back the moment I arrived. This I did, to receive a blistering protest about a story the *Mail* had published that day revealing that Thomson might have to renounce his Canadian citizenship in order to receive a British peerage. Though he did not dispute the possibility, the timing of the story had deeply embarrassed him because of the angry reaction there might be in his native Canada. And he had spotted one inaccuracy for which he wanted an apology. Stalling for time, I volunteered to visit him in his office next morning.

'What hour do you get to work?' I asked.

'About eight o'clock,' he said.

'Sorry,' I replied, 'that's too early for me. I'll call in around nine.'

I then sent for the original copy and saw that a careless sub-editor had altered the text in a way that introduced an error of fact. Calculating that Thomson, for all that he owned a chain of newspapers, had probably never set eyes on a piece of sub-edited copy, I stuffed it into my briefcase. When I was ushered into his office next morning there was no air of welcome about the place. Thomson was at his desk and even his pebble glasses could not hide his annoyance. Beside him stood, almost to attention, his henchman, Ian Coltart. I began by apologising for not realising how much the citizenship story might embarrass him and then produced the sub-edited copy and put it on his desk.

'Gee, what the hell is this?' he asked. I explained that if he read it carefully he would see how the inaccuracy had crept in. 'Great,' he said, 'I guess I've never read copy in its original state before.' When he had finished reading it he dismissed his henchman and said: 'Let's forget all about it, Mike. How are things going on the *Mail*?' I told him what I was trying to do and he said: 'Gee, you're doing a great job there. I love the *Mail*, always have. I still intend to buy it one day.' As we parted, his handshake matched the warmth of his words and I thought what a pleasure it would be to have him as my proprietor. It was a thought that was soon put out of my head when I reported the conversation to Lord Rothermere, who made it instantly clear that he had no intention of selling.

One of the first changes I made to my daily routine on the *Mail* was to abolish the morning editorial conference. At these sessions the home news, foreign, feature, picture and sports editors would go through the lengthy schedules each had prepared, detailing the stories they were chasing, the scoops they hoped to deliver and the names of the reporters, feature writers or photographers assigned to them. Since all departmental heads want to make a good impression, they invariably include in their schedule items that may once have been good ideas (or just dreamed up in the bath) but have little hope of ever reaching the typewriter. My difficulty was to distinguish between the non-starters and the likely runners. To probe, test, challenge and argue with a senior executive in front of colleagues is not a productive exercise. Executives will inevitably feel compelled to defend their claims until their falsity is exposed, at which point the atmosphere may be acrimonious and much time will have been wasted. In place of the morning conference I allocated to each head of department ten, fifteen or twenty minutes of private discussion. Since they no longer had to cut ice in public the resultant talks were so frank and factual that I knew exactly what the prospects were for that night's paper.

Those sessions over, it was time to tackle the mounting correspondence which might include criticisms from outraged readers threatening to cancel their subscriptions ('You can't produce one issue of a newspaper without offending someone,' as Bill Hardcastle once warned me), applications for jobs, invitations to functions, suggestions for stories, submissions of articles, requests for after-dinner speeches or pleas for help from readers in fear of being buried under a mound of bureaucracy. Some of this could be siphoned off to the ever-patient managing editor, Bill Matthewman, who was the editorial administrator. But a sizeable proportion of correspondence had to have a personal reply from the editor. In another tray lay the endless inter-office memos which might relate to which member of the royal family was going to attend the opening of the *Mail*'s annual Ideal Home Exhibition, or what my view was on the current complaint from the National Union of Journalists about the state of the lavatories, the crowded conditions on the editorial floor and the inadequcy of the ventilation system (I have that memo before me as I write and it runs to three foolscap pages). There were also staff expense sheets (see Chapter Four) to be vetted and signed.

After some rapid dictation to highly proficient but poorly

paid secretaries it would be time to read feature articles which were now being processed into early pages, have a word with the cartoonist, and spare some time for a staff member who thought he was being underpaid, before going to a working lunch – maybe with a writer I wanted to hire, a contributor who needed undisturbed discussion (impossible in the office) about how I reacted to his or her writings, a politician, a civil servant, or a group of my executives involved either in present campaigns or future projects. It was over one such lunch that I decided to send Bernard Levin and his column round the world. Out of it came many remarkable stories, but there was one he never wrote for publication until I persuaded him to contribute it to this book. Here it is, as he told it:

In the mid sixties, I was writing a column for the *Daily Mail* five times a week. It was suggested to me that it might be a fruitful idea for me to take my column round the world, filing from wherever I was, with the same frequency. I thought this a most attractive wheeze, planned a journey which eventually took in seventeen countries and set off in high spirits; time-differences, censorship and other nuisances made life difficult, but in the event I never missed a day in the column appearing back home. While I was on the Latin-American leg of my world tour, Kenneth Tynan caused a stupendous uproar in Britain by saying a forbidden word on television. A worldwide – literally – sensation ensued, and where I was the local papers (especially the English-language ones) reported this dreadful affair. But they did not dare (this was, after all, more than twenty years ago) to tell their readers what Ken had actually said; they referred to 'bad language' or 'swearing' and the like.

I was, naturally, much intrigued. A day or two later the US papers arrived; it was even bigger news for them, but they, too, were coy about 'le mot de Tynan', and referred to shock and horror and the like, without specifying the exact offence. I was now choked with frustration, which became considerably more intense a day or two later when the British papers arrived. These had made it front-page news, with enormous banner headlines, *but they, too, avoided saying what Ken had blurted out*. I could stand it no longer, and cabled the London office, demanding to know what he had said. Only after I had sent the cable did I realise that if the answer was rude enough the telegraph authorities would not transmit it. Thoroughly fed up, I put the whole thing out of my mind, and moved on to my next country, which was South Africa.

Now any journalist going on a multi-country tour (indeed anybody, journalist or not) is always loaded with messages from home to faraway friends and colleagues; my notebook was full of instructions to ring Joe in Buenos Aires, and to give Fred's regards to Mary in Bangkok, and the like. So when, in Johannesburg, I got a cable from the *Mail*'s office in London (and having by now forgotten the nine-day-wonder that had so aroused my curiosity) which read 'Ken says if you see Kay give love', I was panic-stricken by an inability to remember who it was who had thus commissioned me, and where and how I would find the mysterious Kay who was to be greeted.

It was only when I was on my way to Kenya that, taking the uninformative cable out of my briefcase and studying it once more, the penny dropped.

Lunches, preferably taken at a leisurely pace though occasionally interrupted by urgent calls from the office (where they were eaten and how they were paid for will be described with relish in a later chapter), were the essential tamers of tensions created by the morning's crowded schedule. They were also builders of the confidence needed to face the exacting demands of the afternoon (show me the editor who eats a sandwich at his desk and I will show you what is wrong with his paper). Back at the office the paper had begun to take shape. Now I must read the last of the feature articles and approve the page layouts, select the political and pocket cartoons from a number of rough drawings, check the progress of running news stories or special investigations, consult with the office lawyer about potential ith the gossip columnist about the main stories, with the riter about subjects for comment and what our attitude e, with the night editor about the early news pages, with the City editor about a story that might be lifted out of the financial pages and projected on the front page, with the lobby correspondent (phoning from the House of Commons) about the weight and worth of the day's political news, with my secretary about the latest arrivals in the correspondence and memo trays, with the managing editor about a bonus I wanted to award for outstanding work and, maybe, with a reporter who wanted leave of absence to sort out his or her love life.

All this was a preamble to the evening conference, held at about 5 o'clock, when we would tentatively dot the i's and cross the t's of that night's issue. Then came the compulsory 5.30 call to Rothermere, which would last for five, ten or fifteen minutes, depending on his mood and preoccupations. With luck he would accept a verbal outline of the as yet unwritten leading article. When luck was out he would insist that, later in the evening, I read to him every word of the completed column, with which he would inevitably find fault. Argument would then lead to compromise. Were I to refuse to listen to, or accommodate as best I could, my proprietor's wishes, demands or, when the going got rough, orders, I would have no alternative but to resign or be sacked. For reasons already stated, I did not regard the leading article as one of the most important elements in the paper and although I intended to, and eventually did, temper its stern Tory judgements with liberal mercy, it was not on my list of priorities. I had already, in my inexperience, wrongfooted myself by exercising what I thought to be the editor's right and, having second thoughts, changed a sentence in the leading article after the writer, George Murray, had gone home. It did not occur to me to consult him on the phone and Murray's furious reaction was to journey to the Cotswolds and complain to Rothermere. Good relations were restored but, if mistrust lingered for a while in Rothermere's mind, the blame was mine.

When the 5.30 call was over I could turn, with some relief, to the emerging paper. Now I could read copies of home reporters' and foreign correspondents' stories, see the proofs of the last feature pages and the earliest news pages, go out to the 'back bench' occupied by the night editor, the chief sub, the page designer and the rest of the technical talent that channelled a fast-flowing torrent of words into the paper. With them I would discuss the disposition of stories, what emphasis they should be given and what pictures should accompany them. I would have a word with the news editor about late developments before returning to my office to deal with the unanswered correspondence and memos. Finally, I would confer with the night editor about the probable contents and shape of the front page. I made it a rule to leave the office by 8 p.m., at which time I could no longer trust my judgement. By then, of course, only half the paper had gone to press and my day's work was not yet done.

Wherever I went, often to the theatre and then on to a restaurant, or to a dinner party, or to an embassy reception, or straight home, the first edition of the paper was delivered to me between 10.30 and 11 p.m. I would spend half an hour or more carefully reading the front page, the inside pages which I had not seen in the office, and the sports pages. I would then go to the nearest phone and spend another half-hour telling the night editor what I thought needed changing, finding out what new stories had come in and how they were being projected, and making notes of what items would need further development on the morrow. Dinner-party hostesses, restaurateurs, and my wife were all immensely patient with this disruptive practice and I can recall only one occasion when it caused offence. At a large party given by Roy and Jennifer Jenkins I was deep in conversation with Lady Pamela Berry (of the *Telegraph* dynasty – later Lady Hartwell) when, out of the corner of my eye, I spotted my host approaching with the first edition. Abruptly, and with only the briefest 'excuse me', I broke off the talk with Lady Pamela, grabbed the paper and retired with it to an empty room. My wife told me later that the horrified look on Lady Pamela's face could only mean that she regarded me as the rudest man she had ever met.

Driven home at last by the overworked but uncomplaining John, I would catch up with domestic news while my wife and I took a relaxing stroll with the dog before retiring to bed in time to put the lights out by 1.30 or 2 o'clock in the morning. In my editing years I survived on five or six hours' sleep a night. The management once attached to me a time-and-motion man who was supposed to tell my masters how I could better organise my working life so that I achieved more in less time. I tried to insist that he followed my every movement round the clock but he was unequal to the task and finally submitted a brief report which said: 'I cannot make any recommendations about Mr Randall because I do not know how he is able to do what he does.' Make what you like out of that, but shed no tears for an editor. He who works hard will also play hard.

8

The Ritzy Life

There were, in the 1960s, twelve window tables in the gilded Ritz Hotel dining room; they overlooked Green Park and were said to be greatly prized by regular lunchers. Why I was allotted one of them I do not know, unless it was that the dignified, courteous, tactful, all-powerful but benign Mr Bishop (styled receptionist but whether senior or junior to the head waiter I never discovered) was also a faithful reader of the *Daily Mail*. It was certainly not because I played the 'Luncheon Game', as described by *Queen* magazine in May 1965. According to the article, which listed the players of the game in six well-known restaurants:

The tables themselves are the real stake ... within every fashionable restaurant there exist status areas and status tables. The thirty tables on the raised platform at the Savoy, for example, are definitely infra-dig. 'My God,' said one of the regulars, 'you're absolutely nothing if you have to eat there.' The twelve window tables at the Ritz are much longed for. Some patrons will go elsewhere if they cannot have them.

The article was accompanied by a diagrammatic drawing which, as I consult it now, reminds me that fellow regular occupants of those tables included Princess Margaret (one remove from me though we never seemed to lunch there on the same day), Lord Butler, Nubar Gulbenkian, Lord Southborough, Norman Collins, John Mills, Anatole de Grünwald, Terence Rattigan, Sir Harold Samuel and Rex Harrison.

Call me economical with the truth or just a typically lying journo, but I did not use the Ritz because it was fashionable (an editor who mixes too much with top people is in danger of losing his detached judgement). I was introduced to it by William Hardcastle, no respecter of high society, and enjoyed its ambience, its impeccable, but not servile, service, its widely spaced tables which ensured that conversations were not overheard by neighbours and, above all, the fact that a *Daily Mail* editor automatically had a signing account (praised be the Lord Rothermere). The staff never needed to be reminded of my simple habits. On arrival in the cocktail lounge I was immediately greeted with an imperial pint of Lanson Black Label and (following Keith Waterhouse's golden rule) the wine always appeared on the table before the food. When the bill came, I added to it a generous tip, signed it and let it find its way back to the *Daily Mail* accounts department where it would be settled without question. Similar facilities were available to me in other London restaurants and I was a familiar figure in many of them (I recommend Chez Victor, in Wardour Street, for liaison lunches), but such was my affinity with the Ritz that when, fifteen years after I had been sacked from the *Mail*, I made my first reappearance there, I was greeted as if nothing had changed and I had never been away. On that occasion I was the guest of the *Daily Mirror*'s Anne Robinson, of whose journalism I have long been a great admirer.

I had always hoped to see a woman become editor of a national daily or Sunday and Anne was my favourite candidate. By 1984 she had become an assistant editor of the *Mirror* and was frequently editing the paper, but it did not give her the same measure of satisfaction that she drew from writing or performing on television. She then made a firm decision not to pursue an executive life in Fleet Street and when, early in 1987, Robert Maxwell asked her to become editor of the *Sunday Mirror*, she declined. As she told me later: 'I realise that I have done nothing to further the cause of sisterhood but you cannot take a job simply because you are the first woman ever to be offered it. The idea of going behind a desk again to spend twelve hours a day there, maybe five or six days a week, filled me with horror. For me it would have been like promoting a leading player in an orchestra to head of accounts and administration. I was, of course, very flattered by the offer but I have no regrets.' Happily I have lived to see two women installed in the editorial chairs of national papers. Wendy Hendry now runs the *News of the World*, Eve Pollard edits the *Sunday Mirror* and, who knows?, the same may yet happen on *The Times*.

When Reginald Maudling left his ministerial desk for the last time he told me that his greatest loss was his chauffeur-driven car. I know exactly how he felt. Just imagine: no more worries about where you will find a parking space, or how long it will take you to hail a taxi when you come out of the theatre in pouring rain, or how much you drank at dinner, or whether the tangled traffic will make you late for an appointment, or what that strange noise is under the bonnet, or when you will find time to wash the car, or by how much your parking meter has overrun its time, or how to get from A to B when your normal route is blocked, or how to change the wheel when the nuts refuse to budge, or why that front tyre is wearing thin, or why the damned thing will not start on a frosty morning, or how you will get it through the MOT. Just relax in the knowledge that wherever you go you will be in a transport of delight, a purring, polished limousine that deposits you at, and picks you up from, your destination at the appointed hour – or, in the latter case, later if you are having a good time. It is, indeed, one of life's greatest luxuries, especially for a technical idiot like myself who has been known, on going through the Dartford Tunnel, to fling his coins all over the road instead of into the appropriate wide-mouthed receptacle.

There was only one occasion when it was not a luxury. Eddy, my chauffeur (worthy successor to John, who had been lured away to drive Rolls-Royces), had just taken delivery of a new white Mercedes, and was proudly waiting outside No. 50, a favourite restaurant in St Martin's Lane. When my wife and I emerged the car would not start. It was a hot night and I had to seek volunteers from the passers-by to help me push the offending car down the road as Eddy tried to start it by the let-in-the-clutch method. Alongside me was a panting man who suddenly exclaimed: 'Good God, I landed here from New Zealand a few hours ago. To think that I have come all this way just to push a bloody Merc through London.' All our efforts were in vain. But Eddy, a cautious man, had not yet handed over the old green Merc, in which he eventually drove us home.

The perks did not end there. Free second-night seats were available for many of the West End theatres; so were passes into the players' enclosure at Wimbledon, tickets for test matches or cup finals, badges for racetracks or greyhound stadiums, seats at the opera, ballet or cinema. On a visit to the *Mail's* New York office my wife and I would fly first class and stay in Lord Rothermere's king-size suite at the Plaza Hotel where vast drinks parties, with five waiters and fifty different canapés, were paid for by signing a piece of paper I never bothered to read (the same went for the expensive doctor who was summoned at 3 a.m. when I was apparently dying of seafood poisoning. He gave me an injection, ordered me to eat porridge for breakfast and had me fit to face the dry martinis at lunchtime next day before I flew along Wall Street, between the tops of the skyscrapers, in a Port Authority helicopter).

In the course of duty I lunched or dined at Buckingham Palace (not one of the better meals, as will emerge in a later chapter), the House of Lords, the House of Commons, various embassies, Guildhall, the Dorchester, the Savoy, the Connaught, Grosvenor House, Claridges, Chequers, City boardrooms, the Admiralty and as guest of the C.-in-C. Home Fleet at Northwood. It was there, at a silver-laden table, that, the Queen having been toasted, I asked permission to smoke from the C.-in-C.'s wife. 'They will be handed round,' she said.

Perhaps the most memorable of all meals was when I was chief guest (i.e. maker of the speech of thanks) at a gastronomic weekend, presided over by the Troisgros brothers from Roanne, at the Imperial Hotel, Torquay. After the Bollinger champagne reception came the *pâté de grives* with the Brouilly 1962, the *sole Albert comme chez Maxim* with the Meursault-Charmes 1959, the *côtes de bœuf au Fleurie à la moelle* with the Chambolle-Musigny-les-Haut-Doix 1955, the *sorbet d'ananas* with the Mérand sweet champagne, the *café* with the Bols dry orange curaçao. After that lot, how could you, as speechmaker, not have them rolling in the aisles? They already were.

The worst line-of-duty meal was at the United States Senate restaurant in Washington, where I cannot recommend the sliced home-cured Senate corned beef. This fleshpot life was, of course, essential in my line of business because from every lunch or groaning dinner table I departed not only with an overladen stomach and impaired liver, but also with an idea (fortunately jotted down on the back of a menu while the mind was still working) for a story or an article.

Both the AA and the RAC made me, as editor, an honorary and therefore non-paying member, while the motor trade in London pressed me to borrow the latest models for the weekend (nothing was asked for, or given, in return). To sit at the wheel of a 130-m.p.h. Ferrari and find that all the drivers ahead of you give way as soon as they spot your approach in their rear mirrors is at once a heady and hazardous experience. I claim (though others may dispute it) that this lifestyle went to my head only once. I took the managing director's advice to have my hair cut at the Savoy. That was one item which could not go down on expenses but I was so impressed, on my first visit, by the way the barber deftly removed, without my asking, the blackheads from my nose that I kept my custom there for years.

Time outside the office was not always spent luxuriating; I had to perform many duties of a more exacting nature. One was to attend the annual dinner of the circulation representatives. The main function of the circulation department is to ensure that the paper, come snow, ice, fog, hurricanes, fallen trees, failed rail signals, broken-down vans, industrial disruption or editorial inability to meet scheduled press times, reaches wholesalers and newsagents in time for them to satisfy their customers. Circulation managers are also expected to increase sales, which they know that they alone cannot do. That does not prevent them from taking all the credit when sales rise and blaming the editor for producing an unpopular paper when sales fall. You may boost circulation by buying the Duchess of Windsor's jewels or the Duke's Buick and offering them as prizes in a competition which is heavily advertised on television, or by revealing the intimate details of what Prince Charles actually says to his plants in those loving talks, but the new readers gained by such ploys will not remain constant unless they like the paper as a whole. The surest way to success is by word of mouth – the 'Did-you-see?' syndrome. To be in a pub and hear one of the tipplers say to a friend: 'Did you see that marvellous piece in the *Daily* — about the hen that laid a square egg?' is balm to an editor's troubled mind. (Incidentally there was a tale in the *Mirror* many years ago about a hen that laid a square egg. The headline was COCK-A-DOODLE – OUCH! When Jack Nener, the editor, saw it he stomped into the sub-editors' room and roared: 'Which of you buggers wrote that?' The man responsible was across the road quaffing his nightly pint or two and his colleagues, fearing that Nener disapproved of the headline, said they did not know who had written it. 'Bugger you, then,' said Nener, 'I was going to give him a bonus.' And that is how Ken Cooper, one of Fleet Street's keenest wits, lost £5.)

Once a year the circulation manager would call all his reps to London for a day of conferring and carousing, ending with a dinner at which they were addressed by every editor in the Associated Newspapers group. Studying the sales reports which the reps sent, with their comments, every week to Head Office,

I realised that many of them were out of sympathy with the kind of paper I was producing. They wanted either more sensation, more sex, more sport or more space devoted to such minority interests as tiddly-winks, underwater wrestling or modelling Buckingham Palace in matchsticks. How was I to convert them? I consulted the circulation director who said: 'First, Mike, you must make the thickheads laugh. They expect a joke every second sentence. But in between the jokes you have to get it into their wooden skulls that they are not selling a carbon copy of the *Express* but a new kind of *Mail*. Win them round that way.' He might as well have assigned me to hell in a handcart. My subsequent failure can be measured by a picture, taken in mid-peroration, which reveals that those of my audience who were not asleep or stifling their yawns, were wearing that limit-of-patience look which means 'pass the port and remember that all bad things come to an end'.

There is in my album another picture which tells a similar tale. The scene is White City, where the *Mail* sponsored a show-jumping event. At its conclusion the editor, who had been given only a minimal briefing, had to walk out into the arena to shake hands with, and make suitable remarks to, the winning riders before pinning rosettes on their horses. There is no hope, on such an occasion, of pretending to be somebody else because that upper-class, riding-to-hounds voice on the loudspeaker is saying: 'And now the editor of the *Daily Mail*, Mr Mike Randall, will ...' Although any resemblance between my language and that of the horsy world is purely coincidental, I could manage the first part of the task. Even if you do not know the difference between a fetlock and a farrier, you can always ask the rider if the seventh jump caused problems and not be thought an idiot (unless, of course, there were only six jumps). But when the girl attendant hands you the first rosette and you have not the slightest idea of where to pin it, and you know that if you take a blind stab at it and the rosette falls to the sacred turf a roar of laughter will engulf the stadium, what in hell (which is where you would rather be at that moment) do you do? In my case you ask the first rider where to put the wretched thing and he, being an equestrian gentleman, will guide your feeble fingers to the right spot. Your ordeal is not yet over because you are then expected to pat or stroke the horse's head. But the horse, a noble and intelligent being, knows an equine ignoramus when he sees one and there is then much pawing of the ground and snorting of the nostrils, causing you to take several steps backwards at double the pace of your cautious approach. Although I was soon proficient in the rosette-pinning technique, I still had to administer the head-patting to three more horses and could only hope that the crowd, anxious for the next event, appreciated the speed at which I completed the ceremony.

Speed was, of course, the essence of Brands Hatch, the Kent Grand Prix circuit where the *Mail* sponsored the Race of the Champions. I was flown to the track in a helicopter which took off from Battersea and landed me in front of the grandstand. What followed was enough to test any man's endurance on his one day off (Saturdays were free from labour but wherever I went on a Sunday I was in constant contact with the office). That endless procession of ever-circling cars, which I wished would disappear up their own exhaust pipes, never seemed to overtake each other (despite the hysterical voice of the commentator, who insisted there was a grim struggle going on for fourth place) and emitted a combination of nerve-racking noise and foul fumes which brought on the inevitable headache (it was either that or the champagne, without which the event was unbearable). When, mercifully, the race was over the then Hon. Mrs 'Bubbles' Harmsworth, who had greeted me by asking why the *Mail* had not carried some marvellous story that was in the *Express* that morning, presented the cup to the victor while my duty was to hand over the magnum of champagne which was duly shaken up and poured over everybody within reach. I found it no easier to talk to a racing driver than to a horse, but I have a great respect for both.

More to my taste were the *Daily Mail* International Jazz Festival (held at Belle Vue, Manchester, in the summer of 1963, and presenting, among many others, Kenny Baker, Kenny Ball, the Temperance Seven, Sweden's Cave Stompers, the Saints Jazz Band, Johnny Dankworth, Ronnie Scott, Acker Bilk, Dizzy Gillespie, Humphrey Lyttelton and Czechoslovakia's Gustav Bron Orchestra) and the 1964 *Mail*-sponsored concerts celebrating Sir John Barbirolli's twenty-first year with the Hallé Orchestra. Barbirolli had launched the Hallé Trust Fund, designed to introduce the adventure of music to more and more people, to give opportunities to young composers and conductors and to take the Hallé – 'this wonderful inheritance of a great city', as Sir John called it – abroad more often. When Barbirolli launched his appeal he invited industry to support the Hallé either by underwriting special concerts or by contributing to the trust fund. Two hours later, due to the urging of our Manchester editor, Harry Myers, the *Daily Mail* decided to sponsor two concerts. To this day I recall with emotion the first of those concerts, in May 1964, when, sitting next to Lady Barbirolli, I reflected on the comparative pettiness of my editing world as I listened to what must have been one of the finest performances ever given of Mahler's Symphony No. 2 in C minor, 'The Resurrection'. And while that glorious music still echoed in my mind there was further delight in store. Now I was host at a Grand Hotel dinner party for Sir John and his wife, Janet Baker and Erna Spoorenberg (whose signatures I have on a treasured menu). Never mind the fresh lobster and salad, followed by the fresh asparagus, followed by the fresh strawberries; think of the man of the night.

Barbirolli was truly charismatic; he had a special divine or spiritual gift. He also had wit, erudition, compassion and a deep care for humankind. He brought to the table a present for the editor – a copy of the *Daily Mail Weekly Magazine* (published on Sundays) dated 30 April 1899. In it there were war memoirs (THE ZENITH OF HUMAN MISERY – AN ASTOUNDING NAR-

RATIVE OF NAPOLEON'S RETREAT FROM MOSCOW), an investigation by a *Daily Mail* reporter who spent a night in cubicle No. 293 of Rowton House (a superior doss house charging 6*d* a bed), an account of a day in the life of Cecil Rhodes, discussions on whether babies can think before they can talk, why women were growing taller and why feminine drunkenness was on the increase, plus advice on the treatment of an ailing elephant (at frequent intervals administer brandy and Rhine wine alternately in doses of half a pint). Nothing changes in newspapers, except names and dates.

9

Word Perfect

'The Queen Mother does it. Sir Alec [Douglas-Home], after cabinets, does it at the back of No. 10. Mr Wilson does it in Hampstead Garden Suburb whenever he has time. Dr Beeching does it, madly, with all the latest devices. And our man next door is always doing it.'

Let us now praise the polishers of first paragraphs, remembering that they are always writing against the clock. The one above is from a *Daily Mail* leading article published on a Saturday (when it was traditionally light-hearted) in 1964. It went on to discourse on the English love of gardening and the Chelsea Flower Show. Leaders are not signed but I suspect the author was Julian Holland. Leonard Bernstein claims the ability to spot a Gershwin composition on hearing the first chord. Similarly I was able, in my Fleet Street years, to name the writer of many a feature article simply by reading the opening paragraph.

News is sacred; the first paragraph must give the knub of the story so that the reader who is pressed for time can, if need be, skip the rest but still have a clue to its main content. Features are free; in them the art of the first paragraph is to take the reader by the arm and invite him to accompany you through the remainder of the article. It is known in the trade as the 'read-me' approach. Here, for example, is the beginning of a news story (from the *Sunday Times* of 12 July 1987): 'The Labour leadership was in turmoil last night after a sudden outburst of hostilities inside the shadow cabinet. The in-fighting, the most bitter since Neil Kinnock became leader, centres on Bryan Gould's rise in the party hierarchy and his call for a new party image and more popular policies.' You hardly need to read the subsequent sixteen paragraphs to know what is going on. But what of this? 'Everybody to his own notion of genius, of course, but high on my list is the man who put "Ah" in front of Bisto.' Thus the late, and much-missed, Vincent Mulchrone beginning, in 1964, an article on the writers of advertising copy. Mulchrone was a first-paragraph perfectionist. Until he was satisfied with those opening words his fingers froze on the typewriter, but when the words swam into his head the rest flowed as smoothly and steadily as a midsummer night's stream. Here is Mulchrone starting an account of the Queen's 1965 tour of West Germany: 'There were serenades and cannonades and small boys falling in the water. They waved balloons from barges and bedsheets from gingerbread castles.' From the same typewriter came these first thirteen words from New Delhi: 'Pandit Nehru was lovingly burned to ashes by his grandson here this evening.' And who but the man whose televised face is now so familiar to filmgoers could have begun a show business article like this? 'Miss Sophia Loren, who lives in the most respectable sin imaginable, was talking about marriage – Italian style.' That was Barry Norman, writing in the *Mail* in 1964.

Even the most experienced player of the guess-the-writer game might be confused about the authorship of the next two examples. The first was written at a party conference in 1961: 'I am no addict to these conference jamborees. The abstract processes of democracy take some hanging on to among the groups, factions, cabals and mutual detestation societies that constitute the arena of professional politics.' The second was penned shortly before the 1964 General Election. 'As polling day comes nearer those of us who have always extolled the British political system as the best in the world can be seen wandering around, with an increasingly anxious expression on our faces, asking passers-by if they would oblige us with the loan of a razor, with which to slit our wrists.' The authors are James Cameron and Bernard Levin, in that order.

There is no mistaking the style of Anne Scott-James who, somewhat before her time, opened her *Mail* column in June 1965 with this:

I plead with the intellectuals of Britain to dam the flood they have unloosed of unutterably banal and repetitive surveys, analyses, essays and interviews on sex ... It is people like Muggeridge, Brophy and Paul Johnson who are drowning us with revelations about sex in marriage, sex outside marriage, teenage sex, middle-aged sex, sex in Scotland, sex in the south-east, sex indoors, sex outdoors, sex at a party and up a tree.

It was left to AIDS to stem that tide.

It must be apparent from the aforegoing that when, in April 1963, I nervously settled my bony bottom into the insecure editor's chair in Northcliffe House, home of the *Daily Mail* until it moves next year to the former Barker's building in Kensington, I inherited no lack of writing talent among my contributors. I also had at my command a fine news-gathering team. I only needed to find the time, within the work schedule described in Chapter Seven, to plot and plan a quiet revolution and steer my enthusiastic staff in a new direction. The *Mail*'s peak circulation in 1961 was 2,650,000 (following the takeover of the *News Chronicle*). In 1962 the figure fell to 2,550,000 and the downward trend was continuing in 1963. One of the penalties paid by the *Mail* for having been the first great popular newspaper in Britain was that many people now regarded it as old-fashioned, while Fleet Street media pundits, led by Lord Francis Williams in the *New Statesman*, unfailingly referred to us as 'the ailing *Daily Mail*', and *The Economist* was soon to describe us as 'vulnerable'. To be dubbed, as I immediately was by *Private Eye*, 'the ageing hack' was irrelevant and, in one part, inaccurate. I was rising forty-four.

My urgent aim was to give the paper a character of its own

which could not be confused with any of its rivals. It was still inclined to ape the *Daily Express*, though not as blatantly as in the days of Arthur Christiansen, the outstanding *Express* editor. (He would introduce a mild change of format in the *Express* and, within a few days, see a similar innovation appear in the *Mail*.)

We could not start again from scratch because we could not afford to cast off any of our old readers (save the 70,000 who died each year). The new character had to emerge gradually so that the impact on the reader was subconscious. I had two main objectives: a greater depth, wider range and higher quality of news coverage with a technical presentation to match it.

I began by laying down a code of practice. It read, in part:

1. No member of the *Daily Mail* staff intrudes, or is called upon to intrude, into private lives where no public interest is involved.

2. No ordinary member of the public is lured, coerced or in any way pressed by a *Daily Mail* representative into giving an interview or picture which he is clearly unwilling to give.

3. It remains our duty to expose the fraud or unmask the mountebank wherever the public interest is involved.

4. In the reporting of divorce cases we use our own and not the judge's discretion. [This was in the days when some publicity-seeking judges used the summing-up to dish out the dirt and capture the headlines.] We give detail only where the case and the summing-up are of valid legal interest or valid public interest. We do not at any time carry reports which merely hold either party up to ridicule or reveal aspects of their private lives which cannot be any concern of the public.

5. No member of the *Daily Mail* invents quotes or uses subterfuge to obtain quotes. The practice of putting a 150-word 'would-you-agree' question on the telephone, getting a rough yes and then writing the whole question as a verbatim of what the man said is not indulged in here. We use no quotes rather than phoney quotes.

6. We are not in business to suppress news that ought to be given. Where anybody is guilty of withholding information that should be

made public we use every legitimate method to give our readers that information.

7. *Daily Mail* staff do not allow themselves to be used as vehicles for the promotion of publicity stunts which have no legitimate news value.

That edict was not altogether popular. Many of the *Mail*'s old hands felt that it greatly limited their scope. But there were many others who were grateful to be ordered to cease practices which they found unsavoury. I went further, demanding that the *Mail* reporters ask 101 questions where others would stop at forty and that individual work should be undertaken painstakingly, with a full understanding of where the paper was going. My unswervingly loyal deputy was Derek Ingram. Together we instilled into everybody our first duty – to inform, at great length if necessary; our second was to interpret. We gave the specialist writers their own columns where they could develop a subject which would otherwise have been dismissed in a few words; we appointed an arts and university correspondent (the latter was Nicholas Lloyd who came to us straight from Oxford and is, at the time of writing, editor of the *Daily Express*); and we persuaded our distinguished Washington correspondent, the late Bruce Rothwell, to return to London and set up 'Newsight', a group of investigative reporters who spearheaded our campaigns against such social evils as the marketing of inflammable children's nightwear, inertia selling (the practice of sending unrequested goods through the post, followed by threats of legal action if they are not paid for), the racialist voice of 'the British Preservation Society', and the sale to the public of the radio pocket spy (later banned by the Postmaster-General).

Derek and I had to convince not only the staff but also the management that, by taking the *Mail* out of the popular and into the quality/popular field, we were on course for success. We were not given great confidence by an incident that took place towards the end of 1963. We had laid down that the reporting of industrial disputes had to be balanced and fair to both sides. This led to our being summoned one morning to Warwick House, Lord Rothermere's London home. We were confronted by an angry proprietor who accused us of slanting the main front-page story in that day's *Mail* in favour of a group of workers who were threatening to strike. All our protests were in vain. Accepting none of our arguments, Rothermere in exasperation charged us with employing a Communist chief sub-editor who had deliberately edited the story so that it was in favour of the workforce. 'If this sort of thing goes on,' he declared, 'I will pick up this phone' (moving his hand towards it) 'and sell the paper.' I did once employ a card-carrying Communist on the *Mail* as an industrial correspondent. But Rothermere never found out. Such wildly impulsive behaviour had, I am sure, medical origins. Rothermere was plainly not a physically fit man at the time and I believe that whatever ailed him had an effect on his mind, which was often in a contradictory state. For example, at one of our regular meetings he agreed with me that a responsible drama critic, chosen for his love and knowledge of the theatre, should not have to pander to public taste but be free to give his personal assessment of play and players. In the next breath he upbraided me for allowing Peter Black, our gifted television reviewer, to cater now and then for minority interests instead of concentrating permanently on the likes and dislikes of the mass audience.

Such proprietorial vicissitudes did not impede the quiet revolution which, in 1964, began to gather momentum – and critical attention. In the office there were many doubters who thought I was aiming too high, letting the idealistic stand in the way of the practical. Sales were still falling and I probably had more anxieties than any of my staff, but if the editor were to show the slightest sign of lack of confidence it would spread gloom through the office. So my professional life became an act and I hid my fears behind a mask of assurance. But within the apparently unflappable man there beat a flapping heart. A commentator in the *World's Press News* (then the leading trade paper) described me at the time in these words: 'He disarms his visitors with his warm yet casual greeting ... He is lithe, restive, always on the run; seldom if ever sits down; yet he is not a top-speed overpowering type of man. One assumes he plays the score by ear. His candour is as disarming as his appearance. This is impeccable, yet unstudied, like the 1964 man – no frills, just the running gear.' And the *Observer* said I was: 'Tall, thin, alert. Manages to keep on the move without looking harassed.' Some act, some deception. The truth is that I played the score not only by ear, but also by hunch, instinct, gut reaction, intuition, impulse and guesswork. I knew my goal, but trod an uncertain path towards it.

The *World's Press News* commentator, Desmond Gorges, went on to make one of the most inaccurate forecasts ever committed to print. His article concluded: 'The *Daily Mail* has a circulation of two and a half million. We won't see it at the three million mark this year or even next. But if Mr Randall has his way and he is correct in his assumptions, there is little reason to doubt that this figure may be obtained not many years from now.' It never was, nor ever will be. Despite the skills of the present editor, Sir David English, with his lively Yuppie appeal and his 'Every Woman Needs Her *Daily Mail*' slogan, the circulation is now below two million.

Nevertheless in 1964 the *Mail*'s method of gathering and presenting the news in a more thoughtful, informative, questioning and interpretative manner was beginning to make its mark. At the same time the campaigns were achieving results. The next step was to devise, by changing the layout and the headline type faces, a packaging worthy of its content. For this I turned to Leslie Sellers, the production editor and a man with a flair for type. As early as May 1963 Sellers had written to me: 'We are in danger of getting too many incompatible type faces as a result of buying in job lots. It would be a good idea to get back to one type family to give us consistency throughout the paper.' What, in lay person's terms, Sellers was seeking was a presentation from front to back which, while it would vary from page to page, would be in keeping with the new character of the paper. Gradually and stealthily, by discarding most of the old type faces and buying a few new ones, by refining and sharpening the layout, Sellers achieved his objective without the reader being aware of what was happening. By then the *Mail* on the bookstalls could not be confused with any other paper.

Together we tackled the final problem. At that time every popular newspaper selected one story each night as the most important or controversial, or sensational or sexy, according to the market in which they were trading. The story, regardless of its comparative merit, would have to appear under a large banner headline, proclaiming it to be of great significance. But no two nights on a newspaper are the same and there are many occasions when there is no story worthy of promotion. By slavish adherence to that technique you cannot avoid giving false emphasis. You are forced to give one story, whatever its quality, four or five times the weight of the next best story. It is a straitjacket from which there is no escape. We set out to evolve a system which allowed flexibility. After months of experimentation we arrived at a format which enabled us to give almost equal weight to two, sometimes three, front-page stories. At first it became widely known as 'Randall's Folly'; in time it attracted grudging admirers. It stemmed from my belief that type should always be the servant of news, never its master. It was also a bid for emancipation from the old restrictive orthodoxy. Since a technical account of what we did would be almost incomprehensible to the lay person, perhaps the illustration over the page best explains it.

There could not have been a nicer compliment on the format changes I was making than when a man in a dirty mac arrived in my office. It was the late Sir William Hayley, a most distinguished editor of whom I was in awe, and he wanted to

Daily Mail

News Chronicle

NO. 21,444   FOR QUEEN AND COMMONWEALTH   TUESDAY, NOVEMBER 16, 1966   PRICE 4d.

Regiment meets death at dawn

As Mr. McNamara, U.S. Defence Secretary, flew into Saigon yesterday America laced mounting Vietnam casualties and new pressure to leave Hanoi. North Vietnam's leading photographer HORST FAAS tells of the battle-described—SEE THEM, South Korea, today

SOUTH VIETNAM'S 7th Regiment died at 8 a.m. yesterday in a sprawling rubber plantation 45 miles north of Saigon.

It died after trying desperately to fight off hordes of Communist soldiers charging in waves through the rubber trees.

On sale to ANYBODY

The radio pocket spy

A DAILY MAIL INVESTIGATION

THE MATCHBOX SPY, the most sinister device yet produced for snooping, has arrived in Britain. And it is being sold to the public.

A Daily Mail investigation has revealed that a device called the Micro-Bug Spy transmitter can be bought in an ordinary TV and radio shop.

The bug fits easily into a matchbox. It can be hidden in an office, house or car, where it will transmit conversations to an ordinary radio up to 100 yards away.

Comment

Too much to do

Probes

In foxholes

Pressures

POP DOLLIES OF BIG L MOVE IN WITH LYONS

THE BIG L fan club of Radio London, the pop pirate ship, is in open rebellion throughout the country in competition with Lyons's Cadbury flavours. Each will have a girl disc-jockey.

Turn to Page 2, Col. 3

3 women die in crash

MP to go

Drug men held

The Queen returns

Bakers call it off, but bread will be dearer

LEADERS of the Bakers' Union decided yesterday to call a one-day "token" strike next Tuesday.

Secrets

Two points

Another MCC fast bowler is injured

ENGLAND fast bowler David Brown has joined David Larter on MCC's fast-growing casualty list.

UMPIRE BARS MCC BOWLER

Rhodesia: MacDonald reports to Wilson at No. 10

MR. WILSON and his Ministers had critical talks last night at the next move over Rhodesia.

Lights cause jams

LATE NEWS

PAGE TEN — Tracking down the Bug

consult me about how to redesign the front page of *The Times*, which was shortly to contain news for the first time.

I could never devote 100 per cent of my time to the production of the paper. There were always extraneous demands. Towards the end of 1963 I was asked to give my views to the Press Council on so-called cheque-book journalism. The Council, a feeble body which has signally failed, on the evidence of today's most popular Press, to maintain, let alone improve, the standards of journalism, wanted to form a policy. The trouble was that they had not defined what constituted cheque-book journalism. The phrase is hopelessly vague and loose since you obviously cannot produce a newspaper without signing a great many cheques. I did my best to make my position clear. On the *Mail* we did not engage in cheque-book journalism if that meant opening our purse to crooks, prostitutes, pimps or the like who were hawking their so-called life stories or inside information; nor did we compete with other papers who used their cheque books to obtain follow-up stories at the end of criminal or divorce court cases, which were often on the borderlines of intrusion; nor did we use cash when we believed that good, honest, old-fashioned reporting would bring us just as good a result. But we had to be free to compete in the open market, and if necessary outbid our competitors, for stories, articles, pictures and serialisation rights which were of valid public interest.

And where did all this rectitude and righteousness (some called it 'holier-than-thou crap') get me? In the beginning, nowhere at all. By the end of 1963 we had lost some 70,000 sales. By the end of 1964 another 50,000 readers had deserted us (while some 250,000 had abandoned the *Express*). On the credit side we had beaten off the new competition from the *Sun*, a revamped version of the old *Daily Herald*, masterminded by Hugh Cudlipp.

The *Sun*, launched as 'the only paper born of the age we live in', rose in September 1964. One of its chief objectives was to put the *Mail* out of business. Long before the launch, first by whisper, then by inspired leak and finally by a powerfully projected publicity campaign, there emerged the promise of, in many ways, the very newspaper that I thought the *Mail* should be. As the propaganda did its work there were plenty of pundits prophesying the *Mail*'s death. Lord Francis Williams put one foot in our grave. The quality Sundays tut-tutted over our fate. On radio and television the commentators were inclined to the Cudlipp view that our days were numbered. And the management at the *Mail* bombarded me with questions: the *Sun* is going to do this, the *Sun* is going to do that. What are you going to do about it? Should we not do it first and spike their guns? My only reply was that we would stay on course and not be deflected one inch from it. We would stand or fall on our merits. Friendly Fleet Street moles fed me a stream of information from inside the *Sun* offices which made it clear that the management had not been able to recruit staff of sufficient calibre to produce the paper they envisaged. This encouraged me, amid management murmurs of disapproval, to go off on holiday to my little house in the south of Spain, there to recharge my brain batteries before abandoning my family and returning to my editorial chair for the week of the *Sun*'s launch.

On the *Sun*'s first night Lord Rothermere, Bob Hammond and Marmaduke Hussey gathered in my office. When the circulation manager brought us copies of the *Sun*'s first edition he told us the paper had gone to press so late that many thousands of potential readers would not see it. Flicking through his copy, Lord Rothermere remarked: 'What a pity. The more people who see how bad it is the better.' How right he was. Thanks to television publicity the *Sun* was bought by three and half million people on the first day. By the end of 1964 the circulation was below one and a half million. We stood, they fell. Within a few months the *Mail* began to take off but, with hindsight, I cannot take the credit. It was all a matter of one penny.

In October of 1964 I learned of a management plan to keep

the price of the *Mail* down to 3*d* while the *Express* and the *Mirror* went up to 4*d* and the *Sun* stayed at 3*d*. Production costs were rising and my concern was that, at 3*d*, we could not afford to produce a paper with enough space to make the fullest use of the *Mail*'s talent, which was seen to its best advantage only in consistently large issues. I wrote a letter of protest to Rothermere, saying in part:

The *Express* shows many signs of having lost its momentum ... Because we are now marketing a product which is clearly different from theirs, I think there has never been a more favourable moment to attack ... To exploit our advantages we need the maximum resources which an immediate price increase could give us. To delay would be to surrender initiative ... If, for example, the customer were offered the choice of a 3*d Daily Mail* with sixteen pages against a 4*d Daily Express* with twenty pages, the *Mail* would be competing under a definite handicap ... I ask that the case for putting up our price immediately – and putting all the money we can spare straight back into the newspaper – be given an urgent and sympathetic hearing.

Rothermere did not reply. But I learned from the managing director that he regarded the price issue as none of my business. Eventually I was assured that, although the price would remain at 3*d*, enough money would be pumped into the paper to ensure that we competed in size with the 4*d Daily Express*. It was – and the story of 1965 is best told in the circulation figures. We entered the year selling 2,368,476 copies a day. By July that figure had reached 2,492,000. After that it sagged, which is seasonally normal for most newspapers, but we finished the year with a higher average daily sale than in 1963. It was, however, the beginning of my end – but before we reach that point there are other tales to tell.

10

Court Circles

One is not invited to lunch with the Queen and the Duke of Edinburgh at Buckingham Palace in the normal way of the social world. There is first a telephone call from the Palace to determine whether, if you were invited, you would accept. Say yes and the formal invitation follows. Say no and that is the end of the matter. I said yes and made my way to the appointed reception room on 26 May 1966. My fellow guests were Peter Dimmock of the BBC, Desmond Ackner (now a law lord), Sir Denning Pearson, one-time chairman of Rolls-Royce, the late Charles Heriot, for twenty-one years the Lord Chamberlain's senior examiner of plays, the late Dame Nancy Parkinson, controller of the Home Division of the British Council, Dr Bernard (now Lord) Donoughue, who was head of the Downing Street Policy Unit, 1974–9, and William Hamling, MP. There was no sign of our hostess or host as we sipped our aperitifs and were entertained by two aides, Major Michael Hawkins and Captain Alastair Aird. At a given signal (I saw not whence it came) we were drawn up in military line. Footmen flung open doors and two corgis entered, followed after an interval by the Queen and the Duke of Edinburgh, who walked down the row, shaking hands and making small talk in the manner of royalty reviewing the assembled ball boys and girls at Wimbledon. When they reached the end of the line we broke ranks, the dogs were dismissed and we moved to the dining room.

My seat at the far end of the table meant that I was, through-out the meal, out of earshot of most of the conversation taking

place between the Queen and the Duke, who sat opposite each
other halfway along the table, and their nearest neighbours.
There was, unfortunately, no general dialogue engaging the
whole table (nor, perhaps, was that possible with so many
guests) and I spent most of my time talking to one of the aides,
who was not one of London's most sparkling raconteurs. The
menu (for *jeudi, le 26 mai*) was *œufs pochés écossaises*, followed
by *selle d'agneau polignac, choufleur au gratin, petits pois à la
menthe, pommes persillées, salade*, followed by *glace au mango*
and biscuits (*sic*). Simple and tempting fare, but I was then
unaware of royal eating habits. Her Majesty was, of course,
served first but tucked into her poached eggs as soon as they
were placed before her. I happened to be served last, by which
time I felt it my duty to throw digestive caution to the winds
and, though I could not now catch up with my hostess who had
a clean plate, at least dispose of the first course as rapidly as
possible so as not to hold up the proceedings. This was made
easier by the fact that my *œufs pochés*, when they reached me,
were almost *froid*.

The admirable purpose of these lunches was to enable the
Queen and the Duke to meet privately, and in a relaxed atmosphere, assorted citizens from many different walks of life. Relax-
ation did indeed come when we left the dining table and took
coffee in the adjoining salon. It was there that the Queen
explained to me how she always read *The Times* backwards,
beginning with the results and reports of the previous day's
racing. She then, with great charm and wit, told me of the
unexpected episode in a foreign tour she had just completed.
At the end of a crowded day the royal motorcade was leaving
the last scheduled stopping place on the itinerary. Because of
the throng of spectators, the procession set out at a cautious
5 m.p.h. and the Queen was not at first surprised or worried
that one woman kept pace with her car and, peering into the
window from behind which Her Majesty was waving to the
crowd, returned her wave with smiling enthusiasm. When,

however, the car began to gather speed and the woman on the other side of the window still stayed alongside it, though her waving had given way to frantic gesticulations and the smile on her now perspiring face had been replaced by a look of despair, the Queen ordered her driver to stop. It was then discovered that the woman's dress was caught in the car door and she had been involuntarily chained to the royal motorcade.

There is another regal tale of a foreign land which was told to me by an unimpeachable source very close to the Queen. Wild editors could not drag from me the name of my informant and 'unimpeachable' sources are often fallible, but I like to think this anecdote is true because I do know that Her Majesty has a deliciously catholic sense of humour. The Queen, on a tour of West Germany, was returning to the royal train when she spotted, under one of the carriages, a number of large silver bowls. Turning to an aide, she enquired about the why and wherefore of them.

'Those, Ma'am,' replied the embarrassed aide, 'are placed beneath the toilet facilities.'

'Oh dear,' said the Queen, 'I do hope they are not collecting souvenirs.'

My lunchtime visit to the Palace was far more rewarding than my previous appearance at that address as a guest at a Garden Party. I was one of the few males to attend in a lounge suit instead of the traditional top hat and morning dress. The reason, in my case, was neither impecuniosity nor eccentricity nor republicanism. It was simply that there was nothing I could hire from Moss Bros that, even with the aid of safety pins, glue or Sellotape, could cling to my misshapen figure. The day was fine, the grounds delightful and the strawberries delectable, but I was not among the selected number who were presented to the Queen. Even if I had been the conversation would, of necessity, have been brief and perfunctory. Firm supporter of the monarchy though I am, I would rather have been on the golf course.

These were not my first royal encounters. It had been my

annual duty, as editor, to be one of the hosts at the opening of
the *Daily Mail* Ideal Home Exhibition. There I stood in line to
receive whichever member of the royal family had honoured us
with his or her presence. Among them, in my years, were the
Queen Mother, the Queen, the Duke of Edinburgh, Princess
Margaret and the then Duchesses of Kent and Gloucester. My
photograph album reveals that what they saw of me, as I shook
hands with a deep bow, was the thinning hair on top of my
head. After the greetings came the procession round the exhibition during which, obeying instructions, I discreetly remained
a few paces behind the royals, leaving them to be accompanied
by higher mortals such as Lord Rothermere, Vere Harmsworth
and the upper strata of management.

I was lucky enough, before I suddenly ceased to go round in
elevated circles, to meet Princess Margaret and Lord Snowdon
socially. My wife and I were invited to be fellow guests at a
dinner party given by Marmaduke Hussey, then a director of
Associated Newspapers, and his always charming, vivacious
wife, the Lady Susan, lady-in-waiting to the Queen. I was
originally ordered to wear a lounge suit because the Princess,
who would be returning to London from the Midlands, where
she was being made an honorary member of the print union,
NATSOPA, would not have time to change into evening dress
before arriving for dinner. Rather late in the day that order was
countermanded because the Princess was running ahead of
schedule. My chauffeur broke the speed limit from Fleet Street
to Richmond and back to collect my dinner jacket in time for
me to make a quick change in the office and arrive, as requested,
before the royals. Princess Margaret had not been in the Hussey
home for more than a few minutes before she asked me to tell
her what NATSOPA stood for. Ashamedly, I could not remember
but dodged the question by pointing to my host and saying:
'There, Ma'am, is a man who spends a large part of his life
negotiating with print unions. He will tell you.' But Marmaduke's memory also failed him, much to the Princess's

delight. (The answer was: the National Society of Operative Printers, Graphical and Media Personnel.)

At dinner I sat next to Princess Margaret and was immediately captivated by her easy-going, unregal manner (though I knew well enough that I must still mind my Ma'ams) and her spontaneous wit. She also shared with me the sinful habit of smoking between courses. The Husseys had hired for the night a woman to wait at table. Her duties included hauling the dumb waiter up from the kitchen, transferring its contents, course by course, to the table, and sending it down again stacked with the dirty plates, platters and cutlery. As the evening progressed it became obvious that the good lady, who at intervals left the dining room, had been sampling the wine and was neither entirely steady of foot nor lucid of tongue. Nothing was said although anxious glances were exchanged around the table. Suddenly the conversation was halted by a great clattering of dislodged china as it went bouncing down the liftshaft in a disorderly fashion. When the cacophony ceased the Lady Susan turned to the Princess and said: 'Now, Ma'am, you know how the other half lives,' to which the Princess replied: 'No, Susan, now I know how *you* live.'

Before we leave the royal, and descend to the political world, a last word on the subject from Ian Jack who sent me this story, for which his headline is NEVER DRINK THE WATER.

I wanted to interview the King of Nepal and had got as far as his personal secretary. 'The King rarely gives interviews,' said the secretary, an urbane man educated, like the King, at Eton (or possibly Harrow), 'but come to the Palace and we can have a talk.' I took a cab from the hotel through the streets of Kathmandu. The secretary and I sat on a sofa in a large, formal room and our talk began, but after five minutes I knew it could not continue. I asked to be shown to a royal lavatory; the first stages of dysentery struck sharply and painfully. I dared not move. After an hour I felt confident enough to emerge, but could find no trace of the personal secretary. The Palace seemed deserted. I wandered around the corridors, took several wrong turnings and at last stumbled into the sunlight and past the Palace guards. I never saw the King, though the next day his personal secretary phoned to say: 'We wondered what had become of you.'

Royalty in this country have permanent jobs; politicians are in temporary work. Thus it was that, from one year to another, I could never be sure who would be coming to one of my political lunches which were held in a private room at the smoothly run Stafford Hotel off St James's Street. I would take with me one or two senior executives and our extremely well-informed lobby correspondent, Walter Terry. He and I had many an anguished discussion about the lobby system, under which an elite group of political correspondents has regular access to the Prime Minister on the condition that not one word of what he or she tells them is quoted verbatim. Hence such tortuous phrases as 'sources close to the Prime Minister said last night'; or 'it is understood that opinion in Downing Street is ...' There was an occasion when Terry, as he confessed, 'went screaming into the night' after a briefing by Harold Wilson. Terry had raised a question about a problem in an African country. The Prime Minister replied with the old standby, 'I'm glad you asked that question,' but he assured his questioner that the British Government was about to launch a great new initiative in that area. When the lobby meeting was over Terry made a few enquiries and decided that Wilson had been thinking on his feet and there was, at the moment, no such initiative, although there might be in the future. Terry eventually returned to the office in a state of distress and asked what he should do if he thought that the Prime Minister was, if not telling untruths, at least taking a liberty with the truth. I told Terry that, so long as he was a member of the lobby and bound by its code, he had to report, in the usual roundabout way, what the Prime Minister had said; but we would, on the following day, run a leading article which raised the doubts we had about the validity of the story.

I had many dealings with Harold Wilson and am not among those who regard him as a devious plotter who set out to manipulate the Press. He was certainly an attentive observer of the newspaper business, an eager cultivator of journalists, and he knew exactly when each of our editions went to press. His timing was astute; he correctly judged the right moment to leak a story or tip off an editor. I had no quarrel with that. All governments try to use the Press in one way or another, often just to float an idea and see how the public reacts to it. It is up to the journalists not to be misled. Wilson did lead me up the garden path once, but I believe it was unintentional. He came to lunch with me during the seamen's strike in the mid sixties. He was convinced that it was all a Red plot. He advised me to send a reporter to an address in London, find out who lived there, await the arrival of a red car (he gave me the registration number) and note the people who got out of it and went into the house. The reporter was dispatched, waited for many a long hour, but the carload of plotters never appeared. After further investigation I published a leading article with the heading IT IS *NOT* A RED PLOT.

Perhaps it is the temporary nature of their employment that makes even the best politicians cynical. The late Iain Macleod was a man for whom I had great respect and admiration. A most liberal-minded Tory, he combined a fine brain with honesty and integrity. Yet when he came to lunch he shocked me. I put to him a hypothetical question: would he feel it right if the Tory Party, fighting a General Election, promised to take *6d* off the income tax knowing that, if it achieved office, the economic situation would make such a cut a hazardous operation. 'Of course it would be right,' he said. 'The most important thing for this country is that it has a Tory Government.' That was honest enough but unconvincing. I did not lose my respect for Macleod and was later to give him a column in the *Daily Mail*. But few politicians make good journalists.

My most enjoyable guest was Harold Macmillan, who refused

to talk politics seriously but regaled us with anecdote after anecdote, told with impeccable timing and marvellous gestures. He was not one to decline to have his glass recharged and when he left the table just in time to return to the Commons for Prime Minister's Question Time I felt anxious about his ability to handle it. I need not have worried. When I checked in Hansard the next day I saw that he had carried it off with his usual articulate aplomb. It was only after he had taken his leave at the end of that lunch that we realised that he was the only politician we had invited who had not given us a story we could publish. But he gave us a good laugh.

11

1966 – and All That

How bright the beginning of 1966; how dark its end. On the night of 7 January the *Daily Mail* was voted Newspaper of the Year by the Granada television programme 'What the Papers Say'. Announcing it on behalf of the judges, Brian Inglis said:

We have often had difficulty in agreeing on the Newspaper of the Year but the verdict for 1965 was clear ... I suppose all of us had qualifications. The *Daily Mail* still suffers occasionally from the effects of split personality. Its general tendency is liberal or even radical. But in times of political upheaval it becomes conservative and even Tory ... There can be no question that it has the most talented bunch of writers in Fleet Street ... The *Mail* has also become a much more socially conscious newspaper with serious investigations into issues of the day. What the *Mail* seems to be doing is moving up to fill the great divide that for so long has separated the popular newspapers from the qualities ... It has a long way to go, but for an all-round improvement in quality it gets the award.

On 11 February I received a letter from Sir Linton Andrews, chairman of the Hannen Swaffer Awards (they are now known as the British Press Awards). It read, in part:

This letter brings you my congratulations on having been chosen by my panel of judges as the Journalist of the Year for 1965. The citation reads: 'For so effectively employing his reporters in bold and imaginative campaigns and exposures' ... I am also delighted to tell you that a member of your staff, Anthony Carthew, has won the award of News Reporter of the Year, and three others have been commended.

The award was not to be publicly announced until the following Saturday morning. I left the office early on Friday evening without letting the staff know of a certain story that was about to break. When the news came in Ted Jeffrey, assistant night editor, started to organise for me a special front page which would go on the presses after the last edition had rolled off them. Friday night is not the easiest time to contact writers whose week's work is done but Julian Holland, the late Marshal Pugh, Monica Furlong, who wrote the agony column, Bernard Levin, Bill Matthewman, who was in charge of administration, Keith McDowall, industrial editor, and the New York office all went willingly to work during the night. Next morning I devoured, with my first cup of tea, a special copy of the *Daily Mail* which, on its mock front page, took the mickey out of me in the most affectionate manner. I was later presented with a framed copy of that page, edged around with the signatures of all the staff. As that Saturday wore on the local telegraph boy wore himself out delivering to my house a succession of congratulatory telegrams. But when the editor's cup runneth over you can be sure that a time bomb ticketh underneath his chair.

Late in February the price of the *Mail* went up by one penny. From *The Times* Sir William Hayley wrote to Bob Hammond, our managing director: 'All good luck at 4d. You are going up on a rising tide. May it long continue.'

To which Hammond replied: 'I hope our timing for the increase is as well grounded as our confidence that Mike Randall will not only hold, but further increase, the sales.'

On 25 February, writing the Press column in the *New Statesman*, Desmond Donnelly said:

The *Daily Mail* went up this week to fourpence. The surprising fact is that it had stayed at threepence so long after the *Daily Express* and *Daily Mirror* had put up their prices on 1 November 1964. The question immediately arises: was the lower price the main reason that enabled the *Daily Mail* to advertise proudly in last weekend's *Sunday Times*: 'Without knowing it, last year 63,789 people were in on the beginning of a trend' [a reference to the *Mail*'s increased sales]. I think not. I suspect that the *Daily Mail*'s circulation will continue to improve at fourpence. My reason for saying this is that I have long believed in the basic theory that the public are intelligent. They are, indeed, much more intelligent than certain publicists realise. Thus it is that the best ad-man in Britain cannot sell a poor product for long ... This same analysis of public commonsense applies to the newspaper business – and Mr Mike Randall, the *Mail*'s editor, is proving it.

But our 'intelligent' readers began to leave us from the day the price went up and by mid-year we had lost 80,000 of them. Perhaps they had been buying the *Mail* because they could get the racecards or the football results for a penny less than elsewhere.

I was soon to join Mr Donnelly in the department of false prophesy. On 6 March, at the Hannen Swaffer Awards lunch, I was formally presented with a gold quill pen and a cheque for £500 (which I soon blued on champagne parties for the management and staff of the *Mail*). To this day I do not know why Hugh Cudlipp vainly tried to stop me giving the traditional speech of thanks, which I insisted on delivering because I had only finished writing it at 2.30 a.m. that day. I had just completed twenty-five years in newspapers and in the course of my speech I said:

The word that means most to me in the award is 'journalist'. During these twenty-five years I have seen doubtful days when the authority of the editor's chair was, in some offices, diminished by the demands of the business machine above him and the unthinking cry for mass circulation all around him. This combination has at times forced some editors to turn aside from the basic purpose of journalism and indulge in all manner of gimmicks, stunts and antics alien to our trade. The less those editors edited the lower became the status of the journalists below them. Today the picture is brighter. Editors everywhere are sitting, if not more comfortably, at least more firmly in their chairs. Newspapermen are producing *new*spapers, the standards of journalists are rising – and with them, most important of all, the status of the British journalist.

After twenty-five years, I should have known better.

On 23 March Lord Rothermere gave a lunch in my honour at Warwick House, inviting the entire editorial staff to celebrate the *Mail*'s growing success. In July he included highly complimentary remarks about the paper in his annual report to the shareholders. On 20 July I set off with my family to drive down to our house in the south of Spain and there enjoy a month's holiday. Stopping the car at Montélimar, in France, to buy that day's picnic, I found it almost impossible, such was the pain, to manoeuvre my body out of the Mercedes. When at last I had done so, it was only to discover that I could not walk a step without support. Bidding the family to go and gather the picnic fodder – and plenty of wine – I remained standing by the car, my hands clinging to the roof. On their return they eased me back into the car which, surprisingly, I could still drive without unreasonable discomfort, partly because it had an automatic gearbox. When I hobbled into our Spanish doctor's surgery he roared with laughter, said I had lumbago, gave me some pills and ordered me to swim.

In my medical ignorance I did not realise that I had slipped a disc.

The pills and the sea slightly eased the pain but when I returned to the office I was still moving not much quicker than the tortoises in our garden. After a fortnight I had to call in a consultant who ordered complete bed rest while I prescribed for myself generous doses of whisky. I lay there for some six weeks, during which the *Mail* won the Newspaper Design Award and I insisted on trying to run the paper by telephone, always having the first edition delivered to me and, after reading it, giving instructions to my deputy, then Arthur Brittenden, who must have found this absentee leadership particularly irksome. No wonder he referred to me in the office as 'the Richmond editor'. Before taking to my bed I had sent Gerald Scarfe (cartoonist of the year for 1965) and Richard West, a feature writer, to Vietnam and I was determined that their combined work should be prominently displayed in the paper at regular intervals. Brittenden, who clearly regarded the project as a waste of space, must have breathed a deep sigh of relief when, at the end of October, I was ordered into hospital for a spinal operation and his 'Richmond editor' was finally silenced by the surgeon. (I had persuaded the NHS to give me a bed with a telephone so that I could continue my remote editing, but I never used it.)

While I was convalescing two loyal members of my staff, who must remain nameless, came to my house to warn me that rumour was piling upon rumour in the office and it seemed probable that I was to be sacked and the paper taken down-market. Together we hatched a little plot to forestall the management. As a result this item appeared in the *New Statesman* on 2 December.

There has been a lot of talk lately about the future of the *Daily Mail*. The policy pursued under Michael Randall for the last year or two was to move it away from the old, failing formula and into the famous gap between the serious and the popular papers. I think Randall deserved – and got, in the various awards he and the paper have won – praise for this. But it was an open secret that the new policy of news in depth and less triviality did not please some powerful figures in the management, and when Randall fell ill a few months ago, Fleet Street rumour-mongers began to whet their knives. It now seems they can put them away. A notice posted [on my instructions] earlier this week at the *Mail* that Randall, recovered, would definitely be returning to the chair on 2 January can only mean he has won his struggle to keep the paper moving along the same lines, and that he can now count on Rothermere's support. Good news: when even the *Daily Express* finds it difficult to imitate the *Daily Express*, it would be a pity to see the *Mail* once again trying to.

At the same time this item was included in Granada's 'What the Papers Say' programme: 'There's good news for the readers of the *Daily Mail* this week ... Randall has been ill for some months and the *Mail* has sometimes shown signs of slipping back into its former role as second fiddle to the *Express*. But he's better and it's been announced that he'll be back at the beginning of January.' A day or two later one of my senior executives phoned to tip me off that if only I would agree to produce a more light-hearted paper my job would be safe. Whether or not he was speaking on behalf of the management I could not tell but I told him firmly that I was not interested in sacrificing basic principles in order to keep the chair.

If there is an art in dismissing people I did not master it. I found it necessary to part company with a few of my staff during my editorship but never without remorse, even though they were well rewarded financially. To tell a journalist that he or she is not up to the job is, even if true, a foul and wounding thing to say. To tell someone, as I once did in all honesty, that he was too good to work for the *Mail* (I was referring to his powerful intellect) is even worse. I found myself in the firing line on 12 December 1966, but I was not prepared for it.

The previous evening Bob Hammond, the managing director, phoned me to say that there were one or two things to be discussed before I returned to the office and he would like to come to my house that night. Taking his words as an indication that my job was safe, I told him that I was in the middle of a dinner party but would happily receive him the following morning when, knowing his tastes, I would have the brandy ready to accompany the coffee. When he arrived there was much friendly small talk until he made it clear that he wished to speak to me alone and my wife left the room. Hammond sat on the sofa, sipped his brandy, fluffed up the carpet with his shuffling feet and said: 'Mike, you won't be returning to the office.' When I enquired why I was being fired I was told: 'Rothermere wants a change of editors.'

I said I was now only too well aware of that but I still had the right to know the reasons for my dismissal.

Hammond said: 'Rothermere does not intend to give any other reason than his wish to have a new editor. Nor does he want to see you.' He then showed me the draft of a management announcement which said that I had resigned through ill health. This I rejected out of hand, telling Hammond that unless Rothermere agreed to see me I would make public everything that had gone on between us. I accepted that I was fired but I wanted Rothermere to do the firing himself, and I intended to tell him to his face that I thought his conduct was as contemptible as his meagre offer of two years' salary in compensation for loss of office. During my editorship, although he had argued about individual items in the paper, he had never made a complaint about my general editorial policy. Indeed, the only letter I received from him on that subject, dated 26 November 1964, said: 'I am delighted with the progress you are making in turning out a really good newspaper.'

I had long ago learned from Gordon McKenzie, my successor as editor of the *Sunday Graphic*, that there are two things you must do when you are sacked: lock up your company car and reject the first cheque you are offered. Rothermere agreed to see me a few days after my ultimatum to Hammond. I left him in no doubt about my feelings and eventually extracted from him one reason for my dismissal. It was the large loss of circulation following the price increase. Reminding him that the pricing policy was his, not mine, I then said that I refused to resign on grounds of ill health, I spurned his cheque and declined to return the company car. He told me that such details should properly be discussed by me with the managing director. I went to see Bob Hammond but the only agreement we reached was on the wording of the announcement that was to be released to the Press that day, 15 December. It read: 'It has been decided to make a change in the editorship of the *Daily Mail* and Mr Arthur Brittenden, at present executive editor, is to succeed Mr Michael Randall.' Financial compensation was still to be negotiated.

Meanwhile both Rothermere and I were invited to appear that night on 'The David Frost Show'. Rothermere immediately declined and I was reluctant to enter into public discussion of my demise so soon after the event. What made me accept was a telephone call from Bob Hammond to inform me that I might well jeopardise the financial settlement if I appeared. That was enough to make me phone Frost and say that I would go on the show provided I had ten minutes with him first to rehearse the questions because I did not want to say anything that might be construed as critical of the *Mail* under its new editorship. Frost agreed, but I was to learn another salutary lesson – about television technique.

When I arrived in the reception room where Frost's guests were given a drink before the show, there was no sign of our interviewer. Growing impatient as screening time approached, I asked to see him and was eventually led to the make-up room where he was being carefully groomed. Frost gave me one minute of his time and outlined three main questions, none of which he subsequently asked me, although he did give me the opportunity to tell the viewers that while editors might come and go with monotonous regularity the staff of the *Mail* was so talented that the paper would not suffer.

The next morning I scanned the newspapers to see what coverage they had given to my departure and, to my surprise, failed to find a mention of it in *The Times*, a paper of the record. It was only when I took a second look at the front page that I saw, to my amazement, that the splash story was headed:

DAILY MAIL DISMISSES ITS EDITOR. The *Guardian* commented: 'Even in a Fleet Street congenitally prone to instant change, instant tragedy, the sad story ... takes some beating ... farewell to three pioneering years of the Randall revolution. One more ritual sacrifice, as usual.' It was some comfort to be given a sympathetic press while Rothermere was harshly criticised, especially by commentators in the *New Statesman*, the *Spectator* and *Punch*. I wish to quote only one writer but must first explain why and how it was Harold Wilson who gave me the article to read.

A few weeks before I was sacked I had received from Downing Street an invitation to spend a night at Chequers, taking with me a few of my senior staff. We were to arrive in time for dinner on Sunday 18 December, and leave after lunch the next day. Obviously I had been invited in my capacity as editor but after I was so rudely incapacitated, on 12 December, I took the first opportunity to phone Marcia Williams at Downing Street, asking her to inform the Prime Minister that I did not wish to come to Chequers under false pretences. Within ten minutes she called back to say that Wilson insisted on my presence. This led the *Observer* to indulge in some inventive journalism. On Sunday 18 December, they published a story under the headline EDITOR TO TELL PREMIER WHY HE WAS SACKED. It began:

Over lunch at Chequers today the Prime Minister will be given a first-hand account of the policy changes in the *Daily Mail* which resulted in the abrupt sacking of the editor ... Mr Randall was invited to the lunch before his dismissal. He offered not to attend but the Prime Minister personally repeated the invitation, indicating that he would be glad to hear whatever Mr Randall wishes to tell him.

The Prime Minister indicated nothing of the sort and I certainly had no intention of burdening him with my personal misfortune.

On my journey to Chequers I was allowed, by special dispensation of the *Mail* management, to be chauffeur-driven for the last time (this courtesy did not extend to the return journey, for which I had to beg a lift). On my way I dropped in on a party being given by my daughter and when I left her house Eddy, my driver, and I discovered that neither of us had brought the special maps sent to us by Downing Street. We lost our way and arrived an hour late. The Prime Minister drowned my apologies with a large whisky and the scene was set for one of the most convivial evenings of my life. It ended at around 2 a.m. when, over the brandy, I failed to persuade Wilson (no doubt partly due to an alcoholically induced loss of articulation) to abolish the lobby system. We were about to retire to bed when Wilson realised that his cat, Nimmo, was missing. There followed a hunt, led by the Prime Minister with all his guests in tow, from room to room until, after some twenty minutes, Nimmo was safely in his master's arms.

The next morning Wilson, his head clearly in better shape than mine, was up and at work long before I descended the stairs. He greeted me with a copy of the *Daily Mirror*, saying, 'Mike, you must read this at once.' It was an article by my old colleague William (Cassandra) Connor and I hope I may be forgiven for quoting it at some length:

Ten months ago Michael Randall ... was selected as Journalist of the Year by the distinguished judges Sir Linton Andrews and Mr George Murray, both of whom have been former chairmen of the Press Council. Their colleague was Mr James Bradley, the general secretary of the National Union of Journalists ...

He won the highest honour that Fleet Street can bestow, made even more renowned by the memory of the unforgettable Hannen Swaffer, who inspired it and in whose memory the award is given.

On Friday Associated Newspapers, who own the *Daily Mail*, announced brusquely that they had decided to make a change in the editorship of the *Daily Mail* ... No reason was given for this sacking, although it was known that Mr Randall had been guilty of suffering from a slipped disc since last August. True, the circulation had been falling after a price rise, but at least four other papers in Fleet Street were also in grave difficulties, some of them more serious than the *Mail*'s troubles ...

Those who made the Hannen Swaffer Award and those who applauded it were doubly right last February. They are still right today. What Swaffer would have said about this dismissal I hesitate to think. But it would have been plenty.

I have a peculiar and selfish interest in the Hannen Swaffer Award – and its newly revealed transient nature – for, when it was first founded in 1963, I won a gong. Now it seems that the honour has become an omen of future ill portent. Gong today, gone tomorrow.

Lord Rothermere is chairman of the *Daily Mail* and General Trust Ltd. I name him Proprietor of the Year.

Looking back on it all, after an interval of twenty-two years, I claim credit for two things: the basset-hound strip cartoon, which I introduced into the *Mail* on condition that the artist, Graham, named the dog Fred, is still running; and Charles Wilson, whose feet I put on the first rung of the executive ladder when I promoted him from reporter to deputy news editor, is now editor of *The Times*.

It was not until 3 February 1967 that the amount of my silver handshake was settled.

Dear Randall, [wrote Rothermere]
I have given the most careful consideration to your position. It was arranged that you will continue to receive the same payment as you received when in office until the end of March. You will then be entitled through your contract to the sum of £22,000, being two years' salary. I have decided to increase this sum of money to £30,000. I send you my most sincere wishes that you will find a new appointment in the near future.
P.S. The Company will be pleased for you to keep your car.

Gordon McKenzie's advice had paid off, but no offers of work had come my way. The only person who sent for me was Edward Heath, then Leader of the Conservative Party in opposition, who invited me to lunch at his flat in Albany,

Piccadilly, where he offered his condolences and I incorrectly forecast that he would lose the 1970 General Election, the subject of much shoulder-heaving when I next met him, as Prime Minister, at the House of Commons.

Later in February I bumped into Denis Hamilton, editor-in-chief of Times Newspapers, at a Press function. He took me by the arm and said: 'Mike, I think I have a job for you – and nowadays we pay proper salaries.' The outcome was that I agreed to join the *Sunday Times* at a salary of £7,000 a year, £4,000 less than I had been earning at the *Mail*.

12

Hurricane Harold

There are as many sides to the character of Harold Evans (in his *Sunday Times* years the most effective editor of our age) as there are to the Rubik Cube. A man of courage, tenacity, generosity and compassion, he also curiously combined diffidence with determination and self-doubt with decisiveness. I have a number of witnesses to his endearing eccentricities and I call first Don Berry, formerly managing editor (news) of the *Sunday Times* and now assistant editor of the revitalised *Daily Telegraph*. Don had been summoned by Harry to discuss a set of pictures. As he entered the editor's office he noticed a frail old lady sitting on the sofa. Harry, who made no effort to introduce Don to his visitor, was standing by the window, intently watching the builders at work on the new *Times* office next door. 'Come and look at this, Don,' he called. Don crossed to the window where Harry pointed to a pile-driver ramming into the earth with rhythmical power.

'Doesn't that do something for you, Don?' asked Harry.

'How do you mean?' queried Don.

'Well, doesn't it turn you on?'

'Oh, I see, Harry. But that wasn't why you sent for me, was it?'

'No, no. Let's have a look at those pictures.'

Their quick conference over, Don left but paused in the outer office to explain to Harry's secretary, Joan Thomas, that he had had a rather embarrassing experience.

'Don't worry about the old lady,' said Joan. 'She's Harry's mother and she's deaf.'

Years later, when Don was leaving the *Sunday Times*, he related that story to colleagues – in front of Harry, who put his head in his hands and said: 'Yes, Don, it's all true. I was mad in those days.'

Don was also present when Harry, at thirty minutes' notice, held what he called a 'futures conference', at which he would listen, briefly, to ideas for special articles or series which might, when publicised, increase the paper's sales. Among those assembled were Jack Sefton, the circulation manager, and various editorial executives, including Magnus Linklater, who later edited Robert Maxwell's *London Daily News* until its sudden death and who is now editor of the *Scotsman*.

'Any ideas?' Harry asked Magnus who, glancing at his scrambled notes on the back of an envelope, replied: 'Well, we're working on this new series about the perfume industry and how a scent can change a man's view of a woman.'

'That's good. That's good,' said Harry. 'Take a note of it, Jack. Women, sex, smells, it's got everything.'

Don interrupted the editor's flow of enthusiasm and asked: 'How will the series differ from the one run in the *Observer* a few months ago?'

'Good question, good question,' said Harry. 'Will it be different, Magnus?'

Looking at the ceiling for inspiration, Magnus replied: 'Well, it, er, it, well ... it will be better.'

Harry turned to Jack and said: 'There you are, you see, it will be better. That's fine then. Thank you, everybody.'

And the conference was over.

My next witness is Lewis Chester, one of the finest investigative journalists it has ever been my delight to know. He has an incisive mind, a deceptively casual approach, a dislike of formality, especially in clothes, and a mountainous mop of hair that is, by nature and not by design, in the Afro style. Here is his testimony:

Early in 1972 Harry said he would like me to come and see Lord Thomson because the proprietor had something interesting to contribute on the subject of Howard Hughes. It appeared that Thomson was well acquainted with Howard Eckersley, leader of the Mormon Mafia which tended Hughes's person and cultivated his money. Like the Mormons, Thomson was a great believer in the Golden Rule. I was keen to meet Roy Thomson because (a) I had never met the old blighter before, although I had worked many years for him, and (b) because I had just started a book (with Stephen Fay and Magnus Linklater) about the bogus Howard Hughes biography (our book was eventually titled *Hoax)*. However, as I was wearing plimsolls and track pants at the time, I asked Harry if we could defer the event until the next day when I could make a more fitting package of myself.

Next day I looked great. Beautifully shaved and combed and attired in three-piece suit of banker-like severity, I was led by Harry into Thomson's sixth-floor office. The editor was halfway across the room when we both saw that the desk-bound proprietor was in a highly agitated state. I could not figure out what was the matter but Harry, more attuned in these matters, cottoned on pretty quick: 'Roy, I'd just like to introduce you to Lewis Chester, one of our brightest ... er ... er ... as you can see, some of the young men do wear their hair a bit long these days.'

'Yeah, Harry,' said Thomson, offering his first words in my presence, 'I was gonna say, he looks like some kind of nigger.'

The rest is anti-climax, though it might be recorded that Harry did not comport himself like the great liberal editor of the age. In fact, he made an excuse and left with blinding speed. Alone with Thomson it became clear that the proprietor was highly nervous. I think he imagined I was a Black Panther come to upset his capitalist applecart. It was only with some difficulty that I managed to assure him that I did work for him, indeed that I was a loyal company servant of twelve years' standing. He talked a bit of Hughes and Mormons, but not with any great enthusiasm. As I left he said, not unkindly: 'I have to tell you, Mr Chester, that if you applied to me for a job with hair like that, you would not find employment.'

Many moons later I learned from Harry that Thomson had told him that I was not under any circumstances to be allowed to interview his precious Mormon mate. As it happened, no conflict arose because I did not fancy talking to the Mormons anyway. Skinhead (by comparison) Fay did that job. The incident, however, left a mark on Harry, particularly when the dustjacket for the British edition of *Hoax* was under consideration. The problem was that he knew that Thomson, who was very interested in the book, would see it and be alarmed by the spectacle of my Afro still flagrantly intact on the back cover. Harry therefore arranged to have the picture of me presented in such a way that I was indistinguishable from my balding colleague, Eric Jacobs, the industrial correspondent.

This is the true insight detail behind Harry's version of having me 'shorn' on page twelve of his book, *Good Times, Bad Times*.

Let us now summon to the witness stand Ian Jack (much quoted in this book for the simple reason that he is one of my very favourite writers). Here is his evidence:

In the late sixties and early seventies, the *Sunday Times* under Harold Evans was marked by its antipathy towards the parochialism of London. It tried to show its readers that we realised that many of them lived north of Watford. Many of the staff came from the provinces – Australia and Yorkshire – and the editor himself was a Manchester boy. Thanks to the Beatles and Albert Finney, the provinces were fashionable at the time. The women's pages, however, continued to resist the change. One day Lucia van der Post wrote that a boutique in Brighton was only sixty minutes away.

'Only sixty minutes from where, Lucia?' I asked.

'Victoria, of course,' she replied.

So much for the plain people of Bolton. But eventually even the women's pages were disciplined by the cultural revolutionaries from up north and fashion captions read 'available from Harrods, Knightsbridge, London SW1', instead of just 'from Harrods'.

That, as it turned out, was the high-water mark of provincial influence. In 1975 I was editing some copy by a young freelance called Tina Brown when I came across a knowing reference to someone 'wearing a Herbie Frogg shirt'. I had no idea what kind of shirt this was but suspected something London and smart. I toyed with the idea of changing the words to 'wearing a smart shirt' and then looked in the phone book and changed them to 'wearing a Jermyn Street shirt'. People in Bolton might reasonably be expected to have heard of Jermyn Street, I thought. The next day I went into the composing room to look for proofs of Tina's piece, only to find them in the hands of the editor, who was secretly re-editing them. Herbie Frogg had been re-instated.

'But Harry,' I said to the man who had insisted on our describing the precise location of Harrods, 'only one in ten of our readers will know what a Herbie Frogg shirt is.'

'Course not,' said Harry. '*Everybody's* heard of a Herbie Frogg.'

Slowly it dawned on me. Harry had fallen out of love with the provinces and into love with Tina Brown. Tina's idea of 'the north' ran no further than Keble College. A few weeks later Harry started wearing contact lenses and threw away his glasses. His shirts changed, too. And some time later they got married.

To divert for a moment but still stay with the subject of provincialism and place names, especially Bolton, another anecdote from Tom Baistow:

W. H. (Bill) Armitt was for many years northern editor and director of the *News Chronicle*. Based in Manchester, he was an archetypal provincial character who never tired of explaining the golden rules of journalism to the staff. One of these was that place names were vital in headlines. 'Never say MILL TOWN FACES RUINOUS STRIKE. The reader wants to know *which* mill town. Tell him BOLTON FACES RUINOUS STRIKE.' (Bill came from Bolton and with his examples somehow worked in a reference to his birthplace, always as the first word of the headline.) One night the town did in fact provide a very dramatic front-page story when a trapeze artist fell from the big top into the audience, killing himself and injuring several others. The story was handled by one 'Mac' MacKintosh, a first-rate sub-editor

with a sardonic wit. After rushing the copy and the headline –
TRAPEZE STAR DEATH DIVE IN BOLTON CIRCUS DRAMA – to the
printer, Mac sent up a joke heading purely for the private amusement
of the stone sub, whose job it is to cut the stories to fit as they land
in the composing room, and to whom it was addressed. Inevitably,
the joke heading got into the first few thousand copies of the paper.
Readers were left in no doubt where the tragedy took place. BOLTON
CIRCUS AUDIENCE FALLEN INTO BY TRAPEZE ARTIST, screamed
the headline in the largest type the *News Chronicle* ran in those
days.

To return to the case of Harold Evans, I nominate myself as
the next witness. I had, you may remember, been hired on
the *Sunday Times* staff (as managing editor, news) by Denis
Hamilton, the editor-in-chief. I had never met Harry but was
invited to lunch with him a few days before I was due to start
work. The meeting place was Wheeler's fish restaurant and I
looked forward to a leisurely and well-nourished discussion of
my duties. Harry, a diminutive, bustling figure, arrived half an
hour late, asked if I was a wine-drinker, ordered half a bottle,
bolted one course and threw me some proofs of a new feature
he was about to start under the general title of 'Spectrum'. I
glanced at them and was about to say that 'Spectrum' seemed
destined to be a dustbin for articles that were not good enough
to appear in other, more important parts of the paper, when
Harry stood up and said: 'Sorry, Mike, got to rush, must get in
a quick game of squash at the RAC. See you next week,' and
was gone.

When I arrived at the *Sunday Times* I had no office, no desk,
no secretary, no telephone. I worked at a table in a room I
shared with my good friend, the late James Dow, who was the
editorial administrator. During my first week in charge of the
news pages I had to handle copy from the famed, Czech-born
Henry Brandon, the Washington correspondent who was, for
reasons I never could fathom, held in much awe and esteem by
the hierarchy. Brandon was the friend of presidents and a tapper

of sources in many high places. Unfortunately his command of English was limited, but he was a proud and prickly man, quick to protest at any alteration of his articles. There was a mysterious routine in the office whereby some senior executive gently doctored Brandon's material before it reached the sub-editors, at which point it was supposed to be sacred. I knew nothing of this and, confronted by a telex which bore a strong resemblance to gibberish, I rewrote it. Frank Giles, the deputy editor who was also in overall charge of the foreign department, saw the proofs of the Brandon article and demanded to know who had rewritten it. I told him and he stomped off to see the editor. Harry came to me and said: 'You've improved it enormously, Mike, but for God's sake don't do it again.'

Now let it be the turn of Cal McCrystal, a most entertaining columnist and formerly an executive in the *Sunday Times* foreign department, to bear witness to the editor's eccentricities. In Cal's words:

When Godfrey Hodgson, himself a former Washington correspondent (of the *Observer*), became foreign features editor of the *Sunday Times* he looked forward to handling Henry Brandon's material from the US capital. He was in for a shock. Brandon's copy was, to say the least, eccentric on account of (a) English not being his first language and (b) a tendency towards imprecision. Hodgson was now in a position to sample the stuff in the raw. When he did so he almost exploded. A witness observed a kind of purple ire moving up from his shirt collar at about the same rate as his incredulous eyes moved down the telexed copy. Then, near to apoplexy, he hurled the offending dispatch upon the floor, picked it up and scrunched it in his hands, flung it floorwards again and jumped up and down on it in great rage. Then he left for lunch. His horror-struck colleague, Nicholas Carroll, picked it up. What to do? If the editor-in-chief got to hear about this sacrilege there would be hell to pay. Nick was not a diplomatic correspondent for nothing. He sent a secretary home to fetch an electric iron which Nick then used to smooth out the rumpled Brandon dispatch. At least, he thought to himself, it is again legible, if not readable.

No one ever discovered why Brandon's difficulty was steadfastly overlooked by his editors. Certainly, he was well connected in Washington, but his scoops were not frequent enough to compensate for his failure to write in a manner that could be understood by the average reader. Harry Evans was well aware of this major flaw in his most highly paid correspondent. On one occasion Peter Wilsher, as foreign editor, pursued Harry round the editor's office, holding a Brandon article in his trembling hands and challenging him to make sense of it. Harry declined.

Harry seldom shirked such major challenges, yet he could be much panicked by minor ones. There was a wonderful example during an editorial conference when warfarin-resistant rats were being discussed. He bore the talk with equanimity until Frank Giles casually mentioned that one should not worry about rats when there were so many mice about. London was full of them, said Frank, particularly Highgate, where Harry then lived. The editor paled and became agitated. 'Mice,' he cried, 'in Highgate?' Frank nodded. Harry's fearful eyes darted from floor to walls, to ceiling, to outside window sills. At any moment we expected him either to jump on to his desk or faint. He was genuinely scared.

This sensitivity could be used against him cruelly. One day Colin Simpson, who had been sent to investigate the terrible trade in ponies exported in ghastly conditions from England to France for human consumption, brought to the office a pony's leg as evidence. He left it in a cardboard box, an unsightly object of blood, hide and hoof. Somebody mischievously mentioned to the editor that Simpson had absolutely conclusive proof for his scandal story and Harry should take a peek at it in a cardboard box in Simpson's office. Unable to resist, Harry went off down the corridor. A small crowd gathered at the other end of the same corridor and waited. It was not so much a scream that came from Simpson's room, more a banshee wail, rising slowly as though from a torture chamber and reaching a peak of such indescribable pain that the half-hidden watchers wilted with shame at the atrocity they had perpetrated upon their leader.

Some of us thought Harry had achieved the perfect defence against mice and severed legs when we first saw him entering the office clad from head to toe in a billowing black diving suit. But this turned out to be motorcycle garb, purchased to go with his 1,000 cc Harley Davidson.

In his forties, Harry dreaded the approach of fifty and the bike was part of his 'must-keep-young' period. I once asked his first wife if she were not as anxious as I that he should be charging around London on such a powerful machine. 'Don't worry, Mike,' she said, 'he'll give it up when it's been mentioned in the *Evening Standard* Londoner's Diary.' It *was* eventually mentioned in the *Standard* and, some time later, Harry *did* give it up.

In the office he was always on the move, frequently at the double. A reporter who had left a half-written story in his typewriter when he went to lunch would return to his desk to find it occupied by the editor tapping out a new version of the story. It was impossible to pin Harry down as he scuttled along the corridor or darted in and out of his office which had two separate entrances; both had to be covered if a successful ambush were to be mounted and a belated answer to a vital question wrung from him. He was not a man inclined to make instant decisions, preferring, perhaps rightly, to keep his options open as long as possible. He may not have coined the phrase 'The editor's indecision is final' but he certainly used it against himself with that curious, but likeable, mixture he had of domination and self-mockery. There came times when I could wait no longer for a decision. To get it I used a special technique: I hovered around until I saw him going into the gents. I would immediately follow, stand in the next stall, and usually get an answer before he zipped up his flies.

Frank Giles was frequently bewildered, if not irritated, by Harry's bursts of frenetic energy, especially when a big probe was in progress. It was during the famous thalidomide (which the erudite Frank always managed to pronounce thalilomide) investigation that Harry, who had gone to the House of Lords to hear the fate of the paper's appeal against an interim injunction temporarily preventing the paper publishing its findings, came through on the phone while Frank was holding the editorial conference. 'Excuse me,' said Frank to the assembled executives, 'but the young master' (as he always called Harry) 'is phoning from behind a potted palm in the Lords.' A few minutes later Frank put down the phone and said: 'The young master has run out of coins. Good. Now we can get on . . .'

There was a strangely prudish streak in Harry, who was in so many ways the radical, liberal, progressive editor. I was to be affected by it before long, but first let us hear from Michael Ward, superb photographer, dazzling entertainer at the piano (moving from classics to jazz with consummate ease), lover of Rolls-Royces which he can no longer afford, and a man who laughs his way through life. Here is his story of Bach on the loo:

On 8 December 1983 I was told by the picture editor to photograph Michel Schwalbé, first violinist of the Berlin Philharmonic, with his Stradivarius. What a pleasant assignment, I thought, what a change from covering riots or fires or boring City magnates. But my heart sank when I learned that I was to do the pictures in Schwalbé's hotel room at the Westbury. Gone were the immediate visions of his face and fingers bowing the strings of his Strad against a forest of other bows during rehearsal. He had not come to London to play but to arrange a series of master classes he was to hold three months later. I foresaw a dull hotel room as background to a middle-aged man in a suit. I was not even sure that he had his Strad with him.

As I went up in the lift I wondered whether, if he had got the violin, he would agree to be photographed in the bathroom, the excuse being that the resonance of a bath made it the only room in a hotel in which one could possibly play a Stradivarius. A small, bespectacled man wearing a suit with immaculate tie and collar let me into a room even smaller than I had imagined. As we exchanged pleasantries I noticed a violin case on the bed and asked if it was the Strad. 'It is,' he replied. 'And what would you like me to do?'

'What,' I asked him, 'is the first thing you would do on waking in a strange hotel room in a strange town?'

'Get dressed,' he said.

'No, no. You would reach for your Stradivarius and play a Bach partita in bed,' I suggested.

To my delighted surprise he said: 'Yes, yes, you are quite right and I have the perfect pair of pyjamas, a sort of gold paisley. I've just bought them.' And he started to undress. He went into the bathroom, returned clad in his new pyjamas, picked up the Strad, sat on the bed and started to play a Bach partita – in his socks. Reluctant to interrupt his superb playing, I gently enquired if he usually wore socks in bed. They were off in a flash, and I hesitantly said that perhaps it might make a better picture if he were actually in the newly made bed. He rumpled it and climbed in.

This is marvellous, I thought, but it is not the bathroom. By now I was bold enough to suggest that, because of the extraordinary resonating qualities of most baths, the bathroom might be the place where he would naturally be playing. 'Yes, yes,' he said, 'much better. I'm always being taken in a suit, this is much more fun.' In the tiny bathroom he tried various positions that would prevent me having camera problems from the mirrors before he finally settled on the lavatory.

It was a wondrous sound and a wonderful picture. Alas, it was not published, being regarded by the editor as unsuitable for a family newspaper.

If there was ever a dull moment in the *Sunday Times* I was not aware of it, peopled as it was by men and women of exceptional talent and unconventional behaviour. The famed 'Insight' team carried out many memorable investigations but had scant regard for either the length of article required or the deadline for it. Consequently their pages frequently went to press after the front page. The redoubtable, pipe-sucking Ron Hall was in charge of 'Insight' presentation. One Saturday night, long after his four pages should have gone to press with a report headlined A WEEK IN THE LIFE OF ULSTER, the head printer measured the type that could not be fitted into the space allotted. It was two yards too long. Hall had the immediate answer. Drawing heavily on his pipe he growled: 'Cut the last two yards and add this,' handing the head printer a piece of paper on which he had scrawled: 'Next week "Insight" will reveal ...' followed by a one-sentence summary of the two yards which had been left out.

It was Hall, incidentally, who, a few months after I had joined the *Sunday Times*, drew me aside in the local pub and said he wanted to talk privately. He was many years my junior and had half my experience. In a confidential tone he said: 'Mike, I just wanted you to know that we have decided to accept you. We realise that you are a professional.' On another occasion, when I was in the process of selecting a new chief sub-editor, Hall advised me: 'The kind of man the *Sunday Times* should recruit is the fellow who would have got a double first at Oxford if only he had stayed at the university.'

Such a man was the brilliantly erratic John Barry, now working in America where he is, among other things, a respected pundit on defence matters. At one time he was chief of the 'Insight' investigators and, in that capacity, he had steered a long hijack report into the paper when it was pointed out to him that there was no reference in the article to the headline which read: ELEVEN MINUTES OF HORROR. Barry was unperturbed. He picked up his pen and inserted in the appropriate place the five necessary words: 'It took precisely eleven minutes.'

At its best 'Insight' was magnificent reporting; at its worst it might produce something like this:

At exactly 7.31 on the dark, drizzly morning of 24 October, four men in green Tiroler Loden overcoats, each sporting the black and red tie of the Seven Hundred Club, emerged from a chauffeured grey Bentley with only 2,000 miles on the clock. For fifteen seconds they stood without speaking on the damp pavement of a mean street in Neasden before turning the black handle of the unlocked yellow door of No. 141.

The Affair of the Twelve Monkeys was about to reach its climactic conclusion.

It had all begun three years earlier when a British ex-convict, who had devoted his years in jail to the study of monkeys, kept a rendezvous with a French sailor in a seedy area of the port of Freetown, in Sierra Leone.

But before we can begin to unravel the countless complexities of the case it is necessary to understand the anatomy and culture of the Barbican Monkey. Only then can we forge together the long chain of apparently unconnected clues that have enabled us to reveal the truth of this bizarre event.

Confronted with such an opening, I would know that the 'Insight' team had no straw for their bricks but were nevertheless determined to produce 5,000 words ending, perhaps, with: 'One thing is certain: only time will tell.'

Zealots carry their own banana skins. Here, once again, is an Ian Jack account of how things can go wrong:

Nobody could really believe there would be a war even when the Fleet set sail for the Falklands. Then the peace talks got nowhere and it began to seem not just possible, but probable. The paper decided it would dispatch more men to the scene. The foreign manager at the time was a young man of mustard keenness and ruthless ambition. One morning I walked into the foreign department with a carry-away paper cup of coffee and a resolve to do my expenses. 'Get a bag packed,' said the foreign manager. 'I've got you booked on a plane to Ascension. The tickets are coming round by messenger.' This surprised me. I thought Ascension was a small island in the middle of the Atlantic, unpopulated apart from the British and American military. The Fleet intended to use it as a staging post on the way south. The foreign manager said I could pick up a ship there.

'I can't believe airlines fly there,' I said.

'Yep,' he replied, 'Branif do. You change in New York.'

Still unconvinced, I looked up the flight number in the world timetable. I had been booked to Asunción, the capital of Paraguay.

Harold Evans was often at a loss to know how to react to the antics of his staff. The late Ian Nairn, who wrote so evocatively of travel and architecture, had a desk in the department known as the Travellers' Arms because Jean Robertson, the resourceful travel editor, had managed to smuggle in a refrigerator which was stocked with the necessary for anyone who required a drop of sustenance from a bottle. Ian had various ways of responding to the ring of his telephone. Came the day when Harry rang and Ian lifted the receiver and said: 'Stoat, weasel and polecat here. Polecat speaking.'

'Is Ian Nairn there?' enquired a puzzled Harry.

'Don't know,' said Ian, 'I'll go and ask weasel.' Harry put the phone down in despair.

I was affected by Harry's prudery when I fell in love with a woman executive on the picture desk, which was run by the late Jack Hallam, a legendary figure who hid his compassionate heart behind a rough, tough manner. If a photographer returned and had messed up a job, Jack would bark: 'You'll find the pistol in my top right-hand drawer.' Yet no one could have taken greater care of his staff. There was a faction in the office which thought that if I were co-habiting (which I was) with a girl who was entitled to express her opinions about which pictures should be selected for publication in my news pages, I would automatically agree with her choice. This was far from the truth. She was forceful, I was stubborn, and we had many a fierce argument about the merits of the pictures. Nevertheless, we were both called into Harry's office where he told us: 'The ghost of Lord Kemsley' (a puritan by repute) 'still haunts this office and I am afraid that the position is intolerable. One of you will have to go.' We decided that she would go, but not for the ungallant reasons which you may be suspecting. Harry offered the minimum compensation of a few hundred pounds. We decided to take legal advice. One phone call from the lawyer and the sum was increased to £2,500. What Harry did not know, because it was not yet apparent, was that my future wife was pregnant and had already decided that it was time to hand in her resignation.

Harry was strangely concerned about pregnancies. Judith Jackson, the motoring correspondent (now on the *Guardian*), was determined to work on as long as possible before the birth of her next child. Harry, ever a keen observer of the female figure, drew her aside one day and said: 'Judith, would you do something special for me?' Judith, thinking he was so pleased with her work that he was going to give her an important assignment, reacted most positively. 'Just be a good girl and go home,' said Harry, 'and don't come back until you have had the baby.'

By way of contrast, here is a pregnant story recalled for me by Anne Robinson from her reporting days on the *Sunday Times*:

You may recall that there was no provision for maternity leave on the *Sunday Times* when I became pregnant with Emma in the winter of 1969. The BBC had maternity written into the house agreement and thanks to yourself and Jimmy Dow (then the editorial administrator) and a lot of kerfuffle, I was allowed three months' paid leave. However, the then news editor, Michael Hamlyn, did not think that pregnant reporters should be treated differently from anyone else and therefore sent me to cover the 1970 Wembley Cup Final crowds when I was eight months gone.

'What happens if I faint?' I asked him.

He puffed on his pipe and said: 'Just make sure you file copy before you do.'

To your credit, Mike, when you heard about it you immediately ordered an office car to race to Wembley and bring me back. Such was equality that while I stood outside the Wembley gates amid the marauding football crowds, Charlie [Anne's first husband, Charles Wilson], then sports editor of the *Daily Mail*, was inside as a guest of honour in one of the posh boxes.

After five years in charge of the news section I agreed to take over the editorial administration of the paper. This involved being a mixture of welfare officer, nominal controller of a £2-million-a-year editorial budget, and negotiator with the National Union of Journalists, for whom I was able to introduce sabbaticals and paternity leave. It was often a rewarding task, especially when I could help a man to find the money to pay for a piano he had bought in an over-extravagant mood, but it was far removed from journalism. Harry compensated me for that by allowing me to write for the paper from time to time. I crave indulgence if I quote from an article which appeared on the leader page in August 1975, because, although it obviously went unheeded, I believe it is still relevant to today's popular Press. I had begun the piece by asking how the then Hon. Vere Harmsworth (now Lord Rothermere), chairman of Associated Newspapers, publishers of the *Daily Mail*, could countenance the activities of Nigel Dempster who, I wrote,

was given a whole page of the Harmsworth tabloid in which to assemble a mass of journalistic clichés while recounting, mainly by innuendo ('was romantically attached to' ... 'the many escorts included'), the sex life of author Lady Antonia Fraser who has been cited by actress Vivien Merchant in divorce proceedings against her husband, playwright Harold Pinter.

Mr Dempster's pretext for writing all this non-news? 'Her name figures glaringly in a divorce scandal – and suddenly her past life has come into sharp focus.'

Let us analyse. Glaringly? As one who has been through the divorce courts twice, I find the only 'glaring' thing about this case is that Mr Nigel Dempster and his fellow glarer, Mr William (anonymous) Hickey of the *Daily Express*, have indulged, and been well paid for indulging, their passion for prying into private lives. 'Scandal?' What, apart from the intrusion of Mr Nigel Dempster, turns a perfectly ordinary divorce case into a scandal in 1975?

And who but Mr Nigel Dempster ... brings 'her past life into sharp focus'? Not you, not I.

I went on to cite other equally nauseous examples from other newspapers, including the contribution of Paul Callan (in the *Daily Mirror*), who listed four of Lady Antonia's friends (all male) and, in obnoxious juxtaposition, quoted her as once saying: 'My favourite exercise is to get my head down.' Towards the conclusion of the article I said: 'Fleet Street is said to be fighting for its economic survival. How much of it deserves to survive?' Harry wrote the headline, A SICKENING WEEK IN FLEET STREET, and Gerald Scarfe's cartoon depicted the evil prying eyes. All to no avail. There have been many sickening weeks since then and, despite the seedy revelations of Press methods in the Jeffrey Archer case, I fear there will be many more.

The time came, in 1977, when, for reasons not unconnected with a costly divorce case, I reluctantly had to take my leave, and a generous redundancy payment, from the *Sunday Times*. By concentrating on foibles and idiosyncrasies, I may have given a false impression of Harold Evans in this chapter. So I would like to end it by stating that he was, without a doubt, the greatest editor I ever worked for. More's the pity that he has been absorbed into the American publishing world. Fleet Street (wherever that now is) has need of him today.

As for me, once more into the wilderness, once more ... but not before I have related how I was invited to leave the *Sunday Times* many years earlier.

13

Enter Maxwell

As I confessed in an earlier chapter, it is not in my impulsive nature to say no to a good offer. Nor do I stop to consider the consequences of saying yes. A more canny character would doubtless have avoided the bizarre, and at times embarrassing, episode that troubled me in the summer of 1969.

On 4 June of that year I was sitting at my desk in the *Sunday Times*, engrossed in reading and correcting a page proof, when I became aware that a bulky black-haired figure was towering above me. I looked up into the penetrating eyes of Robert Maxwell, then a Labour MP and the millionaire owner of Pergamon Press (the publishing firm), and better known now as 'Captain Bob', the proprietor of Mirror Group Newspapers. Maxwell, who had ambled into my office unannounced and without an appointment, drew up a chair on the other side of my desk and boomed: 'Mike, how would you like to edit the *Sun*?'

'I never say no to questions like that,' I replied. 'Tell me more!'

The *Sun* was originally the *Daily Herald*, owned and controlled by the trade union movement. In the 1960s it was an ailing paper and had been bought by the International Publishing Corporation, of which the chairman at the time was Cecil King. IPC relaunched the paper as the *Sun* and, with Hugh Cudlipp in overall editorial control, tried to rid it of its cloth-cap image and boost its sales. King promised to keep it going until 1970 but the circulation remained sluggish and, six months from the day of decision, the paper was reported to be losing £2 million a year. Wherever two or three Fleet Street pundits were gathered together in their favourite watering holes they peered into their glasses and foresaw the setting of the *Sun* – and yet another beery wake.

Shortly before his arrival in my office Maxwell had written to Hugh Cudlipp, who had now succeeded King as IPC chairman, with a proposal to take over the dying paper. Outlining his plans, he told me that under his ownership the *Sun* would at all times support the Labour Party but that he would personally have no say in the day-to-day content of the paper. This would be the sole responsibility of the editor, who would be free to criticise the Labour Party, the movement or the Government whenever he felt such criticism was needed and justified. The paper would be radical, intelligent and exciting. He would publish it on a non profit-making basis and, by increasing the cover price and reducing the staff, would make it economically viable at a circulation of 600,000 copies a day, a modest target.

To my consternation he said he had already spoken to Lord Thomson, then our proprietor, about the possibilities of my being rapidly released from the *Sunday Times* so that I could seat myself in the editor's chair at the *Sun* on 1 July. Maxwell claimed that Roy Thomson was delighted by the idea, had given it his blessing and agreed that I would be taken back by the *Sunday Times* should the *Sun* have to close after a year to eighteen months.

At the end of this strange encounter I told Maxwell that I would consider the editorship but insisted that he should immediately inform Harold Evans, my editor, since his whole approach was highly unorthodox. The next day, 5 June, he phoned to say that he had spoken to Denis Hamilton, our editor-in-chief, who was also delighted and happy that we should have a back-to-back contract by which I would be guaranteed a job on the *Sunday Times* if the *Sun* failed. Denis

Hamilton's memory of that conversation was, as I soon learned, rather different.

Over lunch at the Stafford Hotel on the same day (for some inexplicable reason I picked up the bill), Maxwell told me he was due to go on television that night to discuss his attempted takeover but he would prefer it if I were to be interviewed in his place. I instantly declined and added that I did not want my name mentioned at that stage. Later in the day he phoned from the studios where he was recording the interview with Peregrine Worsthorne to tell me that he had mentioned my name but had said only that I was considering the offer. I replied that I could not deny that and accepted his assurance that he would go no further. No doubt what followed was due to Maxwell being carried away by his natural exuberance, but here is an extract from the transcript of the interview as broadcast:

WORSTHORNE: You say you have got a national Fleet Street figure to edit. Can I press you further? Who is he?

MAXWELL: He is ... the former editor of the *Daily Mail*, Mike Randall, just the kind of man that can and will make this newspaper exciting and imperative reading. He is at present managing editor of the *Sunday Times*, and Lord Thomson and Mr Hamilton have graciously agreed to release him and he is our man.

WORSTHORNE: And he has agreed to toe the Party line?

MAXWELL: No, he has not ... he has agreed to accept the responsibility if the paper comes into being, to be responsible [*sic*] for its editing on an exclusive and sole basis.

Next morning brought the expected summons to the editor-in-chief's office. Denis Hamilton wanted to know what the hell I thought I was doing by making it public that I was to edit the *Sun* before I had even consulted him. I outlined the sequence of sudden events on the previous day and said that I had not doubted the truth of what Maxwell had told me about his consultations with Lord Thomson and himself. I was also able to show Hamilton a copy of a letter I had written to Maxwell on the previous evening in which I said that, while he was free to use my name as a *possible* editor, I needed time to study the proposal in more detail. In particular I wanted to know (a) whether I would be able to have a staff of sufficient quantity and quality to do what must be done editorially, (b) whether Maxwell would be able to secure the necessary union co-operation, and (c) whether the project had a reasonable chance of being economically viable over a long period.

Hamilton then made it clear to me that I must do what I thought best but warned me that any question of a 'back-to-back' contract was a matter for discussion between the two of us. He also hinted that such a contract was unlikely to be granted. We parted amicably and, duly chastened, I went back to my office to brood. The next day Maxwell replied to my letter, saying that it succinctly summed up the conditions on which I would have to be satisfied before making a final decision to accept the editorship – a decision which television viewers would already have assumed to be final. He said he accepted my conditions and looked forward to discussing an editorial budget.

In the following weeks I did my homework and made up my mind about the financial resources required to give the *Sun* Maxwell envisaged a reasonable chance of success. When, in the third week of July, I met Maxwell to discuss my three conditions, I was disturbed by his answers. I was even more disturbed when we subsequently drove in his Rolls-Royce to a meeting with the editorial staff of the *Sun* at which Maxwell asked them to refuse all offers of jobs elsewhere until his negotiations were completed. Hammered by understandably hostile questions from journalists whose paper was under the death sentence and who were not convinced of Maxwell's ability to reprieve it, I could only reply that I, too, needed many doubts resolved before I could advance from prospective editor to the editorial chair.

These doubts were not resolved and, on 25 July, I wrote to Maxwell in these terms:

As you know, I do not question either your sincerity or the editorial concept you have outlined ... You are able to guarantee the *Sun* a life of only one year. That is not enough. As I have already said to you personally:

1. I do not think your budgeting is sound. On the basis of £500,000 new working capital it is impossible for you to ensure out of sales and advertising revenue the £1 million a year editorial budget which would be the absolute minimum required. The competition for the available amount of advertising is going to grow fiercer all the time and the *Sun* cannot be in a highly competitive condition unless it has far greater financial resources than you have in mind. It would be unwise to take any optimistic attitude to advertising when the guaranteed life of the paper is so short and the circulation is on a falling graph. If you were prepared to risk at least £$1\frac{1}{2}$ million ... there would be more belief in the long-term possibilities of the project.

2. The key to Fleet Street's problems is the absurd reliance on advertising as against sales revenue. The ratio at the moment is dangerous and I do not see that you will be able to correct the balance. You talk of a *6d* paper – but all Fleet Street will have to raise its prices next year, which would leave the *Sun* in the same position financially in which it has failed to prosper under IPC.

3. Your forecast that the *Sun* would open with a circulation of $1\frac{1}{4}$ million without any large expenditure on publicity does not stand examination. I see no reason why there should be more than a small curiosity sale.

4. Your market research is inadequate ... and hardly up to date.

You may describe all this, as you did once before, as 'a weakening of resolve'. You know it is nothing of the sort. I have been enthusiastic about your editorial ideas, as many journalists would be. But journalism alone is not enough. There are dreams and there are realities. In my analysis, and I would be happy to be proved wrong, the odds against the *Sun* succeeding under your proprietorship are too long ...

With great reluctance I have to tell you that I can no longer be regarded as prospective editor of the *Sun*, should you succeed in taking it over.

I wish you well and will be more than happy to have these words thrown back in my teeth five years from now.

Captain Bob lived on a short fuse. The explosion came on 31 July in a letter which said that he was shocked and surprised by my decision which was not only incomprehensible to him but likely to cause severe damage to his exploratory negotiations which were going so well. He asked me to reconsider my decision and wait for the accountants' draft report on the project's viability, assuring me that if more money were required he would easily raise it. I remained unconvinced but felt it necessary to refute one accusation in his letter. In my reply I said: 'I naturally cannot accept that my withdrawal now is likely to "cause severe damage to the current exploratory nego- tiations". If the success or failure of your plans is so much dependent upon one journalist, then those plans are not the best founded.'

To this day I still believe that Maxwell's editorial approach was feasible (save for his nonsensical idea that the Leader of the Labour Party should be the chairman of the board). But it was Rupert Murdoch who eventually took over the *Sun* and, at a time when I was still hoping that the standards of journalism would rise, plumbed new depths. I am not referring solely to the over-exposed, over-chested girls on page three, and I am sadly aware that four million readers mock my dismay.

When my skirmish with Maxwell was over I was readily forgiven by my employers for my errant ways and, as I have related, continued to work happily for the *Sunday Times* until chance led me into agriculture.

14

Agricultural Interlude

I was now approaching sixty and, since leaving the *Sunday Times*, had written ninety-two letters of application for jobs. Two-thirds of them had not even been acknowledged; the remainder yielded 'we regret' replies. I had, of course, reported to the Job Centre, only to be politely told they had 'nothing in your line, I'm afraid', and thereafter I had joined the weekly dole-drawing queue. I was not on the poverty line; my redundancy money had been sufficient to settle my debts and provide a small pension. But I could abide neither the idleness nor the inability to make what I regarded as proper provision for my family.

At this time, 1978, we were living in the East Sussex village of Chailey and, as is the way in villages, people came to my rescue. The first was my good friend Peter Low, who was managing a mushroom farm at Longfield in Kent. Would I like to do labouring work for him for a few months? Since I had by then sunk to that stage at which you feel not only unemployable but also unable even to stick another stamp on another envelope because you lack the necessary spittle, I asked how soon I could start. 'Monday,' said Peter. 'Meet me at 6.30 in the morning.'

We had a ninety-minute drive before reporting for duty at 8, at which hour I was introduced to a 20-ton steaming pile of prepared compost that had been dumped in the farmyard at dawn. My knowledge of mushrooms was limited to their culinary delights (have you ever eaten them marinated in olive oil, lemon juice and a bay leaf?) and my acquaintance with compost was purely a nodding one – in other people's gardens. I now know that manure from hard-working grain-fed horses, provided it has the right amounts of droppings and urine and does not have an excess of bedding straw (which should be wheat, rye or barley but not oat), makes the best compost for mushroom-growing, unless an unscrupulous dealer has added water to increase the weight. But at 8 o'clock on that Monday morning I was handed a fork and told to 'get stuck into it'. Alongside the compost mound there was a stack of wooden trays, each 4-foot square and about 6 inches deep, into which I had to fork those 20 tons, ensuring that in each tray the unwieldy material was spread out and levelled so that the density was always equal. As I filled the trays they were taken by fork-lift truck to the pasteurisation shed. By the time we broke for coffee at 10 o'clock, when every ancient muscle in my body was registering a violent complaint at my having abandoned the pen for the fork, it became apparent that the old 'new boy' was not going to demolish the manurial mountain in the required time. Peter came to my aid and, by the lunch break, we had reduced the pile to manageable proportions.

The lunch hour (unextendable) was divided into two parts: twenty minutes with our sandwich boxes, the rest in the nearest pub, where a glass or two of Bass No. 1, every mouthful savoured as if it were Lanson Black Label at the Ritz, soothed the aching limbs and restored the energy for the afternoon's toil.

Once the last piece of compost had left my flailing fork and the last tray had been trucked away, my job was to wash down the yard with a high-pressure hose. A simple undertaking, you might think, and not one to tax either muscle or brain. But there was an art to it. The yard, some 100 feet by 30 feet, flanked by thirteen sheds, was by no means as flat as it looked. It had disguised slopes and curious crevices and was by now littered with thousands of particles of straw and discoloured by oozings from the compost pile. It was essential to learn exactly where to start hosing and how to direct the jets of water so that when you reached the finishing line not one speck of dirt could be seen in crack or crevice. On a mushroom farm, cleanliness comes a long way before godliness. Let your crop catch a disease and you can kiss your profits goodbye. When the yard had been watered and broomed more thoroughly than a hospital ward, the hose was directed on to every tool that had been used that day, leaving them unsoiled and ready for a clean start on the morrow. We knocked off at 5 p.m. but the journey home took two hours for the very sound and simple reason that, whoever was driving, the car always arrived on the stroke of six at the village of Groomsbridge where Peter and I were always first into the Crown Inn for a medicinal thirty minutes.

Tuesday was a day of sexual activity, otherwise known as spawning and casing. The trays that on Monday were filled with compost were now assembled, three at a time, on a bench in the spawn shed where the mushroom seed (or mycelium) had to be forked into, and mixed with, the compost, levelled and pressed down with a tamper, leaving exactly $1\frac{1}{4}$ inches between the top of the tray and the compost. The next process was to spread the casing soil (a mixture of peat and chalk, which is the fruiting medium) on top of the spawned compost before the trays were moved to the gestation shed. From composting to picking, the mushroom-farm lifecycle was thirteen weeks and, in my time, production was at the rate of $3\frac{1}{2}$ lb per square foot. The spawning and casing procedure became, after a few hours, so repetitively boring that I indulged in various fantasies, the best of which was that I was about to fork a human hand out of the spawned compost. I offer the idea, gratis, to any thriller writer who would like to use it in the opening paragraph of his or her next detective story. It was a relief to end the day, as all my days on the farm ended, with the pressure hose, cleaning not only the yard but the entire spawning shed from top to bottom. The boy who has never escaped from my shell still finds joy and satisfaction in squirting vast quantities of water. The delight is doubled when you are being paid for the pleasure.

Wednesday was mainly devoted to repairing the wooden trays which, since they were constantly in use and forever being shunted by fork-lift truck from one destination to another, suffering damage on the way, frequently needed first aid. I once volunteered, at my preparatory school, for carpentry lessons but was eventually advised, if not beseeched, by my instructor to abandon the course when he realised that there was something so defective in my mental and physical co-ordination system that I could no more hammer a nail in straight than I could produce a simple box with four equal sides. My exasperated ex-wives would, I am sure, testify to my inability to fix a plug on to the new toaster without fusing half the lights in the house and then being incapable of (a) finding the fuse box, or (b) locating the blown fuse, or (c), when I was pointed in the right direction, threading the correct bit of wire through the fuse without losing the screws. Such defects run in families. Nobody, not even the Army, could teach my brother Neville to drive a car. He sensibly married a remarkable woman who was not only a superb driver but could also rebuild kitchens, repair lawnmowers and make his suits.

So there I was on a Wednesday, expected to put those trays into a metal jig, unbolt the damaged sides, fit new ones, replace rusted bolts and nail in replacement base planks. Fortunately this was done under the supervision of the ever patient, ever pipe-puffing Dennis, driver of the fork-lift truck and a mechanical genius who had single-handedly constructed the only two specialised machines in use on the farm (see Thursday and Friday). He also suffered from a spine injury caused by having a load of compost dropped on him. Under his tuition, and after he had deftly removed a large collection of bent or crooked nails from the scene of my endeavours, I began, if not to master the task, at least not to make a total botch of it. My reward was to be allowed to deliver a load of mushrooms to wholesalers or retailers (I was never permitted to pick the fungi, a job reserved for the delicate hands of girls and not to be entrusted to clumsy male fingers). Stacking hundreds of baskets of mush-rooms into the back of a large estate car bears no relation to piling in the luggage as you set off on holiday. There is a science to it and, if you do not study it, you end up delivering damaged mushrooms to outraged customers. Luckily, I learned that lesson well enough to be kept as a spare roundsman.

Thursday was my athletic day when I mixed the casing soil in readiness for the following Tuesday. The operation was carried out with the aid of one of Dennis's home-made con-traptions. First, I had to hump a bale of peat on to a bench where I slit it open with sharp knife in a manner which enabled me to manhandle it, a certain amount at a time, out of its plastic bag and, without spilling it, on to a conveyor belt which led up into a large rotating mixer. But as I shoved the peat with one hand so, with the other, I had to mix it with the contents of half a bag of calcium carbonate. Once the bale of peat was empty I had to dash up a ladder to pull a lever which released water into the mixer, then another lever which refilled the tank with the right quantity of water for the next load. That done, it was a race down the ladder to reach the button that stopped the mixer rotating longer than the required time. Failure to pull a lever or press a button at the correct moment would result in my producing (as I certainly did at my first attempt) an unusable slush. I forget how many bags of peat and calcium I had to mix but I do recall that I was up and down that ladder all morning and half the afternoon. After that, it was back to fun and games with the pressure hose.

Friday was mucking-out day. All the trays from which the mushrooms had been gathered had to be emptied of their compost and casing soil and cleaned. I would clamber into a large trailer, there to receive load after load as Dennis operated another of his machines which lifted the trays, one by one, and turned them upside-down in mid-air so that they disgorged their contents into the trailer. As the stuff cascaded around and sometimes on to me I had to fast-fork it to make sure that it was evenly spread all over the trailer floor before the next load landed. When the last tray had been emptied the trailer was driven off to a nearby farm where its contents were left to rot until they could be used as manure. At Friday's end it was not only the trailer, the yard, the trays and the tools that had to be hosed down. By then I had more compost than hair on my head.

I doubt if I would have enjoyed working in the underground Parisian caves where, in 1900, there were 1,500 miles of mushroom beds and some of the caves were so deep that they had to be entered by vertical shafts extending more than 100 feet down into the subterranean galleries and tunnels. But when my time came to leave Longfield (I was temporary replacement labour) I did so with much regret – and greatly strengthened muscles. Today, all those manual tasks I carried out with sweat, toil, fork and backache are performed by press-button automatons – except, I am happy to say, for the hosing-down.

Peter went off to India to build a vast mushroom farm for a maharajah and I went back to the dole queue until I was plucked from it by another local friend, Michael Hardy, who needed help on his raspberry plantation. What do you, who only drive out at weekends to the nearest pick-it-yourself farm and gather the fruit for your freezer, know of raspberries? Commercial picking is a very different proposition. Each raspberry must be of the correct size and ripeness (so that it reaches the market next morning in perfect condition) and withdrawn from its stem with a combination of speed and gentleness quite alien to my fumbling fingers. At the end of my first morning, having furtively discarded hundreds of hand-bruised raspberries, I reported to the storing shed with half the number of punnets that my fellow pickers had filled. By the end of the plucking season I was as proficient as the rest, but then I was sentenced to hard labour. From 6,000 canes I had to root out, with a spade, the dead shoots, leaving the remaining shoots undamaged. After that, it was a pleasure to go down on my hands and kneeling mat and plant 6,000 new canes.

When winter came and there was no more work for me on the plantation I returned to the dreary round of scanning the situations vacant columns and composing ever more unconventional letters of application in the hope that they would at least be read before they went into the waste-paper basket. None of them, of course, mentioned that I was in my late fifties but one of them led me back into journalism. The *Sunday Telegraph Magazine* had advertised a post for which, after an amiable interview with the then editor, John Anstey, followed by weeks of if's and but's, I was eventually, and to my later regret, accepted. Regret? Was I not ecstatic to be back in my old trade? John Anstey was, to put it mildly, a curious man. Every newcomer to his staff, no matter what their past record or their seniority, was engaged on a three-month trial basis. Anstey gave me the title of assistant editor, put me in a large office and, for a whole week, left me alone there with nothing to do but twiddle my idle thumbs. I was summoned to an occasional editorial conference where matters were discussed of which I knew nothing since I had not been involved.

In my second week I decided to untwiddle my thumbs and go in search of work. I made myself known to the features editor and explained my plight. She gave me a few articles to read and briefed me on the office system. Some system! Any articles landing on the editor's desk, be they from regular contributors, commissioned from outsiders or sent in on spec and deemed worthy of consideration, were distributed to various executives whose opinions were sought. Those opinions could not be delivered verbally to the editor but had to be given in signed memos. If you gave a favourable opinion you would invariably receive a sharp memo from Anstey indicating that your judgement was severely flawed and demanding to know how you could possibly recommend a piece so far below the standards of the magazine. Should you look with disfavour on an article you would probably be told that it was just what the magazine wanted. Articles initially rejected by Anstey would be revised to meet his criticisms and resubmitted with a further memo. Thereafter memos would pass back and forth until the article was judged suitable for publication, by which time more than a dozen memos might be attached to it, the last one possibly being from Anstey, reminding you of the faulty judgement you had made in the first place.

Towards the end of my third month I was mounting the steps out of Blackfriars Underground station with, I admit, no great enthusiasm for the day's work ahead, when I felt something go in my back and found I could only hobble into the office, grabbing on the way any support I could find. Next day I had to report that I was flat on my back and would be absent from work until I could rise from my bed again. Anstey's sympathetic reaction was to write to tell me that he had been thinking things over and had decided that the magazine and I were not suited to each other and therefore he did not expect me back at all. In my pain and fury I replied by denouncing his conduct but I had forgotten that, even if I could have risen from my bed, I would not have had a legal leg to stand on because my three months' trial period had not expired and I could therefore be summarily dismissed (this time without compensation). Thus does history, more or less, repeat itself.

The acupuncturist put his needles into me but pronounced me a hopeless case; the faith healer laid her hands on me and admitted defeat. The pain would not go, the limbs would not move. With the aid of airport wheelchairs and a mobile lift to raise me into the aircraft (an odd sort of VIP travel), I flew with my family to Cyprus, there to bask on beaches and soak up the sun, preparing myself for what I knew was the inevitable operation. My brilliant surgeon, E. O. J. ('Curly', but he isn't) Kirwan, refused to put his knife into me until every form of physiotherapy had been tried, all to no avail. I never question my medical masters, believing that they know their business rather better than I do. Kirwan told me that a bone was trapping a nerve and gave me odds of 60–40 in my favour that I would emerge from the operation a mobile man again. If it failed I might be in some way crippled for life. Since I was a cripple at the time I found the odds completely acceptable. My body has been surgically knifed more times than I care to remember, and I was not afraid of another incision. My hospital dreads are of another nature. I entered the ward determined that, after the operation, I would make my own way to the loo before I had to use a bedpan. I believe that is why I was one of the fastest recoverers from a spinal operation to walk out of the Royal National Orthopaedic Hospital. I can still hear the cheers of my fellow NHS patients as I abandoned the stick with which I had arrived and made my way unaided round the ward.

Back home and convalescing, I was again jobless. But not for long. One of my most exciting adventures in journalism lay ahead.

15

Ninety-Day Wonder

In the late autumn of my career, I assisted for the first time at the birth of a newspaper. But chronology demands that we first return to Sussex where, when I had recovered from the spinal disorder, the prospect of renewed idleness was not pleasing. Once again, it was back to the sits. vac. columns and the letters of application. One of those was addressed to Edward Goring who, in the 1960s, was on my staff at the *Daily Mail* as a showbusiness writer. He had been sacked by my predecessor, Bill Hardcastle, but when I took over the *Mail* I reinstated him because I appreciated the humour and satire in his writing as he distilled the gallons of garbage showered on him by the film, theatre and television publicists.

Although life had taught me that one good turn seldom deserves another, I wrote to Edward in the mistaken belief that he was now editing the *Brighton Evening Argus*, a reasonably prosperous regional paper then selling more than 100,000 copies a day. Edward phoned to thank me for the flattery but to inform me that he was, in fact, editor of the *Brighton and Hove Gazette*, a weekly tabloid with a circulation of some 12,000. We met for lunch and he offered me the deputy editorship at the handsome salary of £6,500 a year. Beggars can't be boozers and, since I needed a source from which to pay my wine merchant's bills, I readily accepted.

Having lived my newspaper life in reverse, I still had much to learn. Whereas the normal progression of journalists is from the provinces (where they have a thrilling time covering dog shows, pensioners' parties, village fêtes, horticultural societies, Women's Institutes and the like) to London or other main newspaper centres such as Manchester or Glasgow, I had by chance begun in London and inadvertently worked my way down and out to the provinces. In Brighton I was sharply reminded of how cushioned is the life of a Fleet Street journalist. A rank-and-file sub-editor on Robert Maxwell's *Mirror*, handling a few stories a night (rarely of great length or import), will probably command £27,000 a year, as well as the protection of a resident lawyer who will, or should, prevent them from committing libel. As deputy editor on the under-staffed *Gazette* I frequently found myself combining the functions of news editor, picture editor, chief sub-editor, designer and caption writer, working from 9 a.m. to 6 p.m. and lunching on sandwiches at my desk. The nearest lawyer was at the head office of Westminster Press (owners of the *Argus* and the *Gazette*) in London. No doubt that was the reason, though not an excuse, for my costing the firm, within a month of my arrival, the equivalent of about half my annual salary in settling a minor libel case out of court.

Life on the *Gazette* was not of the kind that makes one look back in laughter. I think Edward Goring sensed even then that he was presiding over a doomed paper, though it was to be in the throes of death for another few years until it was killed off by a weekly freesheet, launched by the same company. Try as he might (and he seemed, on average, to try something new once a fortnight, a tribute to the fertility of his mind but hardly conducive to a consistent newspaper) there appeared to be no method by which Edward could halt, let alone reverse, the slide in the sales. So perhaps it was not surprising, given such a forlorn task, that the editor underwent a character change on his way to work. At his bachelor dinner table he was a charming and generous host, an accomplished cook, a wit and a raconteur with a love, and considerable knowledge, of literature, music and drama. Yet when he arrived in the office, hung up his leather jacket and lowered his tightly trousered bottom into the editorial chair, his wit was apt to give way to biting sarcasm and his charm to icy scorn for the efforts of his underpaid staff.

Ironically, after forty years in the trade, it was on the *Gazette* that I was initiated into the new technology of newspaper production, not the completely computerised version now in use in many centres but, at the time, revolutionary enough for me to have to prove that an old dog can be taught new tricks. Years before I left Fleet Street the equipment was available to, if not already installed in, national newspaper offices but, blocked by the printing unions' resistance, was unused until Eddy Shah at *Today* and later the unnecessary, regrettable, foolhardy battle of Wapping broke through the union barriers.

It was a meeting of the National Union of Journalists in North Road, Brighton, that gave rise to the best story ever to come out of the building which housed the *Argus* and *Gazette* – the Mystery of the Bugged Canteen. Apart from being the provider of subsidised meals for the staff, the canteen was also used by journalists and printers, separately, for their regular chapel (local union branch) gatherings. It had for some time puzzled officers of the NUJ that, when they met management the morning after a union meeting, the bosses were remarkably well informed about the previous evening's discussions and resolutions. At first the officers suspected a mole among their members but then the incredible rumour spread that the canteen was bugged. A detecting device was procured and, at the next meeting, it located a bug hidden high in the wall. Next day journalists and printers went on strike, refusing to return to work until management had satisfactorily explained the presence of the evil eavesdropper. Such was the gravity of the affair that a senior union official came down from London to address the strikers. At a fiery meeting she persuaded us to return to work on the understanding that the rest of the building would be combed and a full enquiry held into the planting of the bug, the head of the investigating team being an independent party.

The enquiry established beyond doubt (not that we had
that the canteen had been bugged but failed to nail the cu
The law of libel prevents me from giving an opinion but I
still regard it as highly unlikely that, as one management man
suggested, the printing union was bugging the journalists or
vice versa.

After eighteen unmemorable months on the *Gazette* I learned,
rather late in the day, that Charles Wilson, whom I had appointed deputy news editor of the *Daily Mail* in the mid-1960s,
was gathering staff for a new Scottish quality Sunday paper
which he would edit. I phoned him in Glasgow. 'Mike,' he said,
'why didn't you call sooner? I've filled all the best posts, but
there's one that might interest you. Can you fly up for lunch on
Friday? Good, you'll find the ticket waiting for you at Gatwick.'
I flew, lunched, was hired and returned home in time for dinner
with the news that I was to be production editor of the *Sunday
Standard*, which would be launched by George Outram (a
subsidiary of Lonrho), publishers of the *Glasgow Herald* and
the *Evening Times*. I was returning, at last, to the kind of
journalism I had thought I would never experience again but I
did not then know that I would also be working with a clutch
of companions so large in heart and generous in friendship that
I would, to this day, shed for them the last drop of Scotch in
my veins.

Charles Wilson, Glasgow-born, was short of stature but long
on potency, with a forceful presence that jabbed at you and a
well of energy that never ran dry. He made his points in short,
sharp bursts of shotgun speech, laughed as easily as he swore
and was as compassionate as he was demanding. He was also
a permanent punter on the horses and the only man I know
who, setting off on his first honeymoon, stopped the car at the
nearest betting shop. Nobody but Charles could, from conception through gestation to bawling birth, have seeded, mid-
wifed, nursed, nourished and cradled that paper child in ninety
days. But he would probably agree that he could not have done

it so well without the aid and skill of his page designer, John Ryan, a man for all journalistic seasons. Heavily built, his trousers undecided about whether they should hang from above or below the bulge, his round, pug-nosed face expressing mirth and despair simultaneously, J.R. had supreme confidence in his art and ability, as well he might. He designed (or 'doodled', as he always called it) through flair, instinct and intuition and, when necessary, at a speed I doubt any Fleet Street layout man or woman could match.

I joined the paper, in 1981, only a fortnight before the first issue of the *Sunday Standard* appeared on the Scottish news-stands, but, through John's eyes, I can relate one part of the fast-moving story of the preceding seventy-six days. The association between Charles, then editor of the *Evening Times*, and John, then working on the *Daily Record*, had begun two and a half years earlier when John was painting a ceiling in his house in East Kilbride. Summoned down the ladder by the commanding ring of the telephone (an instrument no journalist can afford to ignore, day or night), he heard this: 'My name is Charles Wilson. You don't know me but I know about you and you know about make-up. When can we meet? . . . Fine, and how will I recognise you?'

Said John: 'I'm overweight, I've got short white hair – and I always wear a green carnation' (not true but John was a literary man with a Wilde sense of humour). They met and John was hired as assistant editor to redesign the *Evening Times*.

Two years later, John was leaving the Albion Street building one evening when he bumped into Charles who asked: 'What are you doing tonight? Can you come home with me? I want to talk to you privately.' When they arrived at Charles's house in Crown Gardens, the editor, as was his wont, publicly removed his lounge suit trousers and replaced them with denims. Pouring the drinks, he said to John: 'We are thinking of launching a new quality Sunday paper. I want you to go away and draw up the book' (meaning the merest outline of the paper showing what size of advertisements and what editorial content there would be on each page) 'and don't let anyone know what you are doing.' John doodled and delivered, Charles added more regular features and soon they had the basis of a 32-page broadsheet. Time passed, John heard no more of the venture but he was given a tempting offer to rejoin the *Daily Record*. He sat up all night deliberating and finally wrote out his resignation from the *Evening Times*. Next day he was approaching the office when Charles, sitting in his company Rover listening to a horse-race commentary, flashed his lights, indicating he wanted to have a talk. They went up to Charles's office where John handed over his letter of resignation. 'Eff that,' said Charles as he tore it up.

On 22 January 1981, the first of the ninety days, Charles said to John: 'Right, there's an office for you on the fourth floor. Get in there and organise the wire services, fix up freelances, find a gardening correspondent, contact all the publishers and hire book reviewers.'

'What about doodling?' asked John.

'No effing time for that now,' said Charles.

But nothing could stop John drawing – laterally. He believed the reader should not be confronted with columns of type that wandered up and down the page at length but should be presented with shorter columns spread wider across the page with clear demarcation lines dividing one item from another. The result, in the Scottish market, would be a paper in appearance as distinctly different from its competitors as the *Independent* now is from the rest of the London dailies.

You may visualise and draw as many specimen pages as you like but eventually they have to be put to the test, translating the pencilled designs into 'dummies', setting headlines and stories in the designated types, reproducing pictures and advertisements and pasting them all up into complete pages. Only then can vision be judged with precision. When, some sixty days before the launch date, John was ready for the first test, he discovered that his problems were only just beginning. He went to Charles who told him: 'It can't be done in this office. The compositors won't set a letter, a comma or a dog's cock' (trade description of an exclamation mark) 'until they have finished negotiating the price for their work. And that's a long way off. Go anywhere in the world to get it done. How about New Zealand? I'll leave the decision to you.' John had to find an established paper using the same Harris input system by which the *Sunday Standard* was to be produced. He consulted the production department and decided on what he believed to be the *Newport News* in Virginia, America. He called the systems manager, Henry Jackson. Could he come over and set up some pages?

'Yep,' said Henry, 'whenever you like.'

'I can't find the *Newport News* in *Willings Press Guide*,' said John.

'That's because it is a town in Virginia,' replied Henry, 'where we produce the *Times Herald*.'

They agreed on a date and John reported to Charles who said: 'Why are you still here then? What flight are you on? ... Well, book one fast and take an assistant.'

John, who hated flying, took the overnight sleeper to Euston, his precious page designs packed into an outsize artist's bag which, being on the short side, he had to carry at shoulder height to keep it off the ground. Next day he and his assistant, Bill McGregor, landed at Norfolk, Virginia, hired a car and set out for Newport News, only to be stopped for speeding, their Scottish accents so intriguing the traffic cop that penalties were waived.

The following morning they were at the *Times Herald* offices where the typesetting was soon done but there appeared to be a technical hitch over producing proofs of completed pages.

'Not sure if we can do that for you,' said Henry Jackson.

'We'll pay anything you like to get them done,' said John.

'Don't want your money,' replied Henry. 'Go back to your hotel and leave it with us.'

John and Bill were at dinner when the call came to tell them their pages were ready. They abandoned the meal and returned to the *Times Herald* to see the disastrous results, the pages bearing scant resemblance to John's designs. It seemed that the electronic make-up system was so programmed that it could not faithfully reproduce the layouts. Tired and deflated, John and Bill returned to the hotel. John phoned Glasgow to explain their predicament.

'Computers only do what they are told,' growled Charles. 'Try again.'

Next morning Charles was on the phone again, his voice ominously quiet.

'How are you doing, John?'

'Still trying, Charles.'

'What column widths are you working to?'

'Eight columns to a page.'

'Well, can you do eight editorial columns to a page with advertisements that are based on a ten-column page?'

To a page designer this is an aesthetic horror, but technically feasible. The reason for Charles's request was that the *Glasgow Herald* was a ten-column paper and many of the advertisements it carried would also be appearing in the *Sunday Standard*, lifted from one paper to the other unchanged in size or content. The solution was the use of 'bastard' measures, setting the type at less or more (or a combination of both) than the normal column width to fill the space between the ads and boldly ruling off that section from the rest of the page.

The following afternoon Charles called again and the ensuing cross-purposes conversation took place.

'Where the hell are you, John?'

'In Virginia, America.'

'What are you doing there?'

'You sent me.'

'Well, for Christ's sake get back here fast – like now. I've got problems with the column widths, problems with the unions and I need you here. Can you get the shuttle to New York, then BA to London?'

'OK, Charles.'

But it was not OK. It was George Washington's birthday and America was shut. The last shuttle had gone.

'Don't worry,' said Henry Jackson's secretary. 'I've got a friend in an airline. Go to Norfolk airport and he'll get you to New York.'

John and Bill drove to Norfolk but there was no sign of the secretary's friend. Bemoaning their plight in expletive language and in volume for all the world to hear, they were approached by a man who asked: 'Are you guys desperate to get to the Big Apple? I'll fix it. Wait here.' They waited until another man, in uniform, arrived and said: 'You the guys for New York? Thirty bucks each.'

John proffered some extra bucks as a tip but the man said: 'Hell, no, I'm the pilot,' and led them to a twin-prop plane with eight seats and no loo. They reached New York late at night, caught the first plane out to Heathrow and the shuttle to Glasgow where Charles wanted to see the pages.

'Christ,' he said, 'I don't want them to look like that.'

'Nor do I,' said John, 'but you pulled us back before we could get them right.'

It was now fewer than fifty days to the launch. Charles had been hiring staff, among them a highly professional, totally dependable, imperturbable character, by name Bill Merrifield and by disposition a man for the fields, the wildlife, the hills and the open air (of which he was to see very little for the next two years, though he cultivated plants in the office).

'You and Merrifield will have to go somewhere else to get the pages done,' said Charles.

John went back to the production department where he was advised to try a firm called IFRA (experimental pioneers of new forms of printing) in Darmstadt, near Frankfurt, West Germany. 'They'll do anything you want. Contact Wolfgang Schneider.'

Said John to Bill: 'We're off to Germany tomorrow. Pack your bags. I've booked the flight.'

Said Bill to John: 'But I don't fly, *ever*.'

'Get me a map. We'll drive,' said John.

John reported to Charles who said: 'It's up to you if you want to drive but you leave now, not tomorrow.'

John to Bill: 'Fill up the car and grab some pictures from the library.'

They drove through the night, caught the ferry to Ostend and, sleepless, carried straight on to Frankfurt where, as soon as they had checked into their hotel, John designed a few more pages.

Next morning Wolfgang Schneider said: 'Sorry, we are just a conference centre here. We don't set any type. Never mind, we'll find a jobbing shop.'

He took them to a one-man business where the one man said: 'Sorry, I can't set the type but I'll do the pictures – let's have them.' Bill had grabbed the first batch of pictures that came to hand in the library and had not even looked at them. He now fished them out of his briefcase and found, to his dismay, that they were all pictures of Nazis.

'A good joke, *ja*?' said the one man.

But there were no hard feelings and, the pictures done, they moved on to an industrial estate where they met an enthusiast called Herr Gutfreund (Mr Goodfriend, which he certainly was).

'Ach, yes,' he said, 'we used to do this sort of thing. I'll dust down the old machines.'

Hundreds of headlines and stories were set and the paste-up artists went to work to prepare the page proofs. Unfortunately they had their own ideas about how it should be done and what emerged was not what John had envisaged. John persevered, pleaded and coaxed until things began to take a better shape.

After a few days Charles was on the line from Glasgow.

'John, why don't you fly back to meet Mike Randall?'

'You mean the man who put the split headlines on the front

page of the *Daily Mail*? What's he got to do with us?'

'He's just agreed to join us.'

'Christ, how old is he now?' (a perfectly reasonable question since I was then sixty-two).

'Never mind about that. He'll be at my house on Sunday morning and I want you to meet him. But I'd like you to bring what pages you've done on Saturday.'

It was Friday. John flew to Glasgow, leaving Bill to carry on with the pages, and drove to Solway to join his wife at their weekend rented hideout, arriving late at night. Next morning he drove back to Glasgow and delivered the pages to Charles who gave him the good news that he would soon be able to arrange for page proofs to be prepared in the Albion Street office.

'You look tired,' said Charles. 'Don't drive up again tomorrow, I'll send a hired car for you.'

On Sunday morning John's car broke down and he arrived an hour late. The champagne was flowing and the pages were spread all over the dining table. I was asked for my comments, and I said how much I liked them but that I felt they lacked any element of surprise.

'I don't want any effing surprises,' said Charles.

John reached for a glass of champagne, his first. He was smartly tapped on the drinking arm by Charles.

'You haven't got time for much of that,' he said. 'You've got to get back to Darmstadt.'

Charles relented, gave John a 24-hour break at Solway before he flew back to Germany to resume his 'doodling'. With fifteen days to the off, John and Bill drove back from Darmstadt. By now it had become possible to produce dummy pages in the *Sunday Standard* office, where I arrived fourteen days before the launch.

16

Excuse Me ...

And so it came to pass that in my sixty-third year I, known to my new colleagues as Father, left my Sussex home every Tuesday morning, took wing from Gatwick to Glasgow, laboured five days, climaxing in a 9 a.m. to 1 a.m. Saturday stint, snatched a few hours' sleep and caught the first plane out on Sunday morning, returning in time to join the regulars at noon in the Five Bells, at Chailey, which was then run by 'Gorgeous' Joe Cornelius, the former star of TV wrestling, from whom I learned into what part of his opponent's anatomy the artful wrestler is liable to stick his thumb.

I had to wrestle with one or two problems when I joined the *Sunday Standard*. Although, when I edited the *Daily Mail*, my reputation stood higher in Glasgow and Edinburgh than it did in London (where there are more disparagers, detractors, derisers, cynics and sneerers per square mile than in any other city), many years had passed and it became clear that I would have to prove, to Scottish journalists and printers alike, that I still knew my trade. There were only a few staff members from south of the border and I occasionally overheard a complaint about 'bloody Sassenachs coming up here and pinching Scots' jobs'. Jumping that hurdle, I landed on the firm ground of friendship, which I soon put at risk when, in a pub round of ten people, I opted out of the eighth drink. I was not to repeat that mistake whatever the consequences, which included, one night, finding myself in a stranger's house stroking a snake as it curled its way round my neck and returned to my lap. I recall, though the memory may be unreliable, that what I thought would be slimy and scaly was smooth and silky. According to a 1987 Press Association survey the Scots (of whom there are only some five million resident in their native land) spend £3.5 million a day on alcohol, more than they pay out on clothes, cars or maintaining their homes. Educated as I was (professionally speaking) in the liquid schools of Fleet Street, it was left to Glasgow to confer on me an honorary degree in C_2H_5 OH.

Money flowed like printer's ink in the early days of the *Sunday Standard*. The firm paid my air fares, booked me into the North British Hotel with a signing account, gave me liberal expenses and a book of chits that entitled me to free taxis at any hour of the day or night. The time came when I had to pay my own way in planes, digs and cabs (when I left I had trebled my overdraft) but for the moment I was back in the happy routine of hard work followed by hard play.

The work, in the first seven of the fourteen days before the launch of the paper, involved recurring hours of trial, error and ever more trial. The layouts of the feature pages had already been settled. John Ryan and I, with the help of wee Albert, the paste-up man, now had to produce a string of specimen news and sports pages, writing endless mock headlines, trying out various type sizes, experimenting with all the possible variations of the lateral make-up and submitting the results to Charles Wilson who, quite rightly, sent us back again and again to the drawing board until he was satisfied that we were evolving the correct designs for a quality paper with popular appeal. There came an evening when John and I, tired, tense and frustrated by all this make-believe, yearning for the real thing and reassuring each other that we would get it right on the night, threw down our pencils, stamped on them and went out for a few healing drams.

We were spotted in the office car park by Charles, who yelled: 'You two effing idiots. Where do you think you're going? You haven't got time for drinking now. And where's wee Albert?'

'We've sent him home, Charles. He needs a break.'

'Go and get him back. And do some more pages.'

Under verbal fire we retreated to the office, feeling like two schoolboys caught bunking a class. Fortunately, it was too late to recall Albert. We had our drams and were forgiven in the morning.

With only seven days to go, Charles announced that all the production staff would be confined to the office for the weekend, visits from wives or girlfriends being strictly forbidden. Like a squad of footballers in pre-match training, we spent the Saturday pretending to produce a newspaper, going through all the motions but unable, at the conclusion of our phantom labours, to hold the finished product in our hands. On Sunday Charles rewarded us for our imaginary efforts by holding a convivial conference at Loon Fung, then the best Chinese restaurant in Glasgow, where the succulent dishes on the revolving hot plate were as numerous as the circulating bottles. Lunch over, we disbanded, free to resume our sex lives or otherwise ease the tension of what lay ahead. The Sunday paper working week normally begins on Tuesday but we were back at our desks on Monday morning, knowing that the dress rehearsals were now over and opening night was 120 hours away.

Charles had assembled, in ninety days, a formidable staff and an impressive list of contributors. Among those who wrote for the first issue were Ian Aitken, political commentator, Ludovic Kennedy, lamenting that 'Nanny England' will rule Scotland for ever, Alistair Maclean, on the unexpected subject of human rights, Derek Cooper on the art of living, Katie Stewart on cookery, Allan Massie on television, Neville Garden on music, Mike Tomkies on wildlife and Peter Alliss on golf. Staff members included Thomson Prentice, now science correspondent of *The Times*, Sally Magnusson, who was to become a television personality, Ian Archer, award-winning sports writer, Sally O'Sullivan (Charles's wife), who was women's editor and now runs *Options* magazine, Norman Mair, rugby correspondent, John Bell, currently city editor of *The Times* and Ian Stewart, prize-winning photographer whose pictures now enhance the sports pages of *The Times*.

Charles alternately coaxed and castigated us. He knew exactly what he wanted from his staff and how to get it, be it by cajolery, nursing or berating. He had three favourite sayings: the first began with a deceptively gentle 'excuse me', abruptly followed by a harsh 'what the effing hell' as he grabbed a reporter by the shirt collar, confronted him nose to nose and demanded to know why vital questions were left unanswered in the offender's story; the second was 'Can I borrow you for a moment, darling?' (addressed to man or woman) which prefaced a private talk in his office where he would consult, praise, thank or encourage his visitor, often asking if he or she had any problems or worries; the third was 'I *am* the editor', when discussion, debate and argument had gone on long enough and decisions had to be taken and adhered to. My only serious disagreement with Charles was when, perhaps out of devilment, he strongly advocated the case for introducing bingo into the paper. My ethical nerves snapped as I hotly denounced the whole lottery business as one of the evils of modern journalism. Under Charles, of course, *The Times* later introduced Portfolio (top people's bingo) and I now begin each day in high hopes (always dashed) of winning a few thousand pounds as I check my golden card.

Although my title was production editor (Charles bestowed it on me to preserve the dignity of his ageing former editor), I was, in reality, a sub-editor from Tuesday to Friday, sitting at the table where all the feature pages were designed, the articles edited, or largely rewritten if necessary, and the headlines devised. I sat beside John Ryan, for whom I sometimes deputised as designer, never matching his innate skills. Feed him headlines to which he responded, giving him at the same time the lengths of the articles he had already scanned, and, with a few thrusts of his pencil, he would outline, in five minutes, a page which perfectly reflected its contents, the type always being the servant of the words. Should he amble grinningly into the office, as he often did, two hours late when we were already behind schedule, he would crack a few jokes, flip through the morning papers, chat to colleagues about anything but work and then go 'doodling' on the drawing board to such effect that by the day's end we had fulfilled our work quota. There is a confidence in some people that reduces the hectic to the leisurely. John had it.

Opposite me sat Jackie McGlone, the tiny Newcastle girl with the outsize spectacles, incisive mind, the rapier wit and the miniature electric fan which she placed on her desk to ward off the offensive smoke that constantly was emitted from the male mouths around her. She had been in newspapers long enough not to be offended by the language that issued from those same mouths. Her neighbour was Bill Fitzgerald (known as Hulk), a lovable, gentle giant with an unpredictable temper which, when it flared, could soon be doused by a few gins and tonics. He was a radical and an anti-establishment man; it was hard to persuade him to enter a pub where he might encounter senior editorial executives or members of the management. He was also the only one of us who did not have to scratch his head over Danny Kopec's chess article, checking it by playing every move on his own board. When I last saw Hulk he was talking in a pleading voice to the computer on his desk, begging it to do his bidding and not keep arguing with him. The fifth member of our team was Bill Merrifield, the soberest and sanest, who kept his cool by growing tomatoes on the window sill.

Since we were the ones who received whatever came off the typewriters or out of the cameras, and processed that material into pages, we were known to the rest of the staff as the Lego Squad and our table was called Legoland. Many of the writers, either attracted by the ribaldry with which we relieved our tensions or curious to see how we were handling their copy, became regular visitors to Legoland. Among our favourites was the debonair Clive Sandground, the diarist who, after a few 'dear boy' salutations would, at around noon, flick his fingers and say: 'I must go and move my car.' We did not then expect him back for about four hours, knowing that he was 'seeing a few contacts', a euphemism for a protracted lunch. On Saturdays we all assumed different roles in another part of the office where the pace quickened as the news pages followed each other in rapid succession to the presses. Since I was nominally production editor it fell to me to draw up an over-optimistic schedule that was supposed to lay down the order in which the thirty-two pages should be completed, thus, in theory, ensuring that the paper went to press on time. But such are the vagaries of journalists and the caprices of journalism that, as the week went by, the schedule had to bow to the wind of change and become as flexible as Labour Party policies since the last election.

As, in that last week before the first issue of the *Sunday Standard*, the hours to the deadline ticked all too rapidly and remorselessly away, my anxieties mounted until they reached a stage at which I wished I could temporarily remove my head from my body, lay it to rest for a while and be free of its swirling, panic-laden thoughts. I would wake each night in my hotel bed muttering to myself that I was too old for the task and what the hell was I doing in Glasgow and did the Scots really want a quality Sunday paper anyway. (On the latter question I was not comforted by my friend the ever-attentive hotel barman who, when I explained what I was doing and described to him the up-market aims of the new journal, replied: 'Aye, I see, a bit like the *News of the World*.')

It was the thought of my responsibilities on the coming Saturday that drained my confidence, causing me to concentrate only on what could go wrong. My duties, in fact, would be quite straightforward. Once the last of the feature pages was completed, I would assume the role of chief sub-editor, handing out the news stories to the various sub-editors, telling them what lengths to edit to, what types to use and how the headlines were to be set, at the same time making regular checks on progress, ensuring we were keeping pace with the clock, and regularly visiting the composing room where the pages were pasted up. Since our sub-editors were recruited from the *Glasgow Herald* and the *Evening Times* and were unfamiliar with our style, stories inevitably over-ran their allotted space and had to be instantly cut or fell short and had to be padded out, the lateral layout not permitting the use of 'fillers' (very short items) to plug the white spaces.

By the Friday night sleep, that blessed obliviator of obsessions and pardoner of sins, totally eluded me. On the morning of 25 April 1981, I walked with hesitant steps across George Square towards Albion Street, my briefcase weighing uncommonly heavy in my twitching hand, my mind envying the feeders of the pigeons, the early shoppers and the folk who strolled at the pace of people whose week's work is done. I was later to learn that I was not the only one who had not closed an eye in the night (Charles Wilson was another). Tension pervaded the office but relief was at hand. We began the day with a glass or two of buck's fizz, and went to work with a will, and no time for doubts now. A quick conference to discuss the merits and dispositions of the main news items, the final sub-editing touches to the last feature pages, and down we trooped, clutching our wire baskets, laden with copy, rulers, pens, pencils, type-books and the ever-necessary coffee mug, to the 'back bench' (where sat the editor and his production team). First down was Charles Wilson who, when I arrived, was engaged in what I assumed to be an important telephone call, possibly to Mike Hatfield, our man in Westminster. In fact, such was his sanguine temperament, he was calling his bookmaker.

Lunch, strictly teetotal, was taken at the desk and one of the secretaries earned more of her salary by making coffee than by typing. (Many Saturdays later, John Ryan's heavy frame slumped to the floor at the most hectic part of the afternoon. We all feared a heart attack but the hospital doctor, at first mystified, finally diagnosed that the eighteen cups of coffee he had drunk that day had made him keel over. He was back in time to enjoy the end-of-work session in the pub.)

I encountered only one unforeseen hazard on that first Saturday. There was a pub so close to the office that it was almost part of the premises. The Scots being an enlightened race, and the pub being a workers' watering hole, it had an industrial licence and was therefore allowed to remain open all afternoon. Some of the printers spent their 'tea-break' there and occasionally a paste-up man, who had to use a scalpel with skill and speed to cut up the columns of type which came out of the system on sheets of bromide, would, with unsteady hand, lop off the first letter of every line, rendering whole paragraphs unintelligible.

One or two of us on the 'back bench' had need of that pub when, having disposed of all the inside news pages and having had no respite since 9 a.m., we felt the urge, at around 4 p.m., to restore the energy required to tackle the all-important Page One. 'Just going to clean our teeth, Charles,' we would say to the editor, who warned: 'Go easy on the mouthwash.'

There was a front-page crisis on that first Saturday night. The main headline read: KGB SPIES 'STILL AT WORK IN WHITE-HALL'. The story under it reported allegations by General Sir Michael Gow, commander-in-chief of the British Army of the Rhine and a former head of Intelligence in Germany, that Britain's diplomatic and security services were still harbouring highly placed KGB agents (*plus ça change . . .*). There were other good stories on the page (and Ernie had obligingly awarded that week's £100,000 premium bond winnings to a Scot) but we lacked a picture with sufficient impact. Charles summoned Arthur Foster, the picture editor.

'What have you got for the front?' he asked.

'Nothing special at the moment,' replied a despondent Arthur who had been relying on pictorially dramatic shots of a pulp mill at Fort William, about which we thought we had an 'exclusive' story – until it broke in the *Daily Record* that morning and no longer merited the main illustration on the page.

'For eff's sake,' said Charles, 'you've had ninety days to get a front-page picture. Where is it?'

John Ryan came to the rescue. 'Give me all the pictures that have come over the wire,' he said. Discarding shots of African heads of state, beggars in Sri Lanka, beach scenes in America and Aborigines in Australia, he alighted on a picture of snowbound sheep. John had read a story which began: 'Sheep-farmers in south-west Scotland, faced with their biggest financial disaster for many years, dug through snowdrifts yesterday to try to rescue their buried stock. Thousands of sheep and lambs were suffocated or frozen to death in the freak Arctic blast ...' Further down the pile John came across a picture of police going to the rescue of a car and caravan trapped in the April snow. 'That's it,' said John, as he began to design the page. 'We'll tie in these two pictures with the weather story and away we go.'

Charles choked and was momentarily speechless. When he could again give tongue he exploded: 'Eff that. Weather and sheep at the top of the front page of this new quality paper? Are you trying to destroy me, John?' But nothing pictorially better arrived before the deadline and the snow-fleeced sufferers remained on the front page.

When the first copies of the first edition of the first issue came off the presses and into our impatient hands the euphoria precluded all self-criticism. Charles had wisely put a ban on alcoholic celebration at that hour because there were more editions to produce. But he sneaked me an outsize Scotch, saying: 'I think you need this, Father.'

John Ryan summed up our exhausted emotions at about midnight. 'Christ,' he said, 'to think we've got to do all that again, fifty-two bloody weeks of the year.'

There were, of course, imperfections in that first issue but in the ensuing weeks and months we produced an ever-improving paper. It never, alas, hit the circulation target of 175,000 copies a week (optimistic in a country of only five million people) and there came a time when Charles called John and me into his office and said: 'Take it seven per cent down the market. You're Legomen, I leave it to you.' John and I conferred. He said: 'I'll put the headlines up a size,' and I said: 'I'll take the verbs out of them.' Thus 'BLIZZARDS BRING DISASTER TO FARMS' would become 'FARMS IN BLIZZARD DISASTER' (twenty-nine letters reduced to twenty-three). A few weeks later Charles called us in again. 'Down another two per cent,' he said. John and I conferred. 'Oh, God,' we both said and carried on as we were.

The end came in 1983 when Lonhro would no longer tolerate the financial losses, but before that Charles had left to join *The Times*, where he soon became editor, and I had, through an old man's pride, returned to Sussex. Albion Street was never the same after Charles had left us, handing over to his very capable deputy, Jack Crossley (many years ago my valued news editor on the *Daily Mail*), but I missed the fiery leadership, no matter how exacting it had sometimes been. Jack now had to choose a deputy and I was on his shortlist. I desperately wanted the job, and felt I was perfectly equipped for it, but, no doubt due to the span of my years and the length of my lunch hours, I was denied it and resigned, thereby missing a handsome pay-off cheque when the closure came. In my last week at the *Sunday Standard* my colleagues allowed me hardly an hour's sobriety, so many were the farewell lunches and dinners they gave me. I returned home with, most appropriately, a beautiful and capacious cut-glass decanter, a present from all the staff, and a silver wine cooler from 'his friends on the Lego Squad'.

Thereafter I rejoined the *Brighton and Hove Gazette* (now defunct) and transferred, after eighteen months, to the *Mid Sussex Times*, in Haywards Heath, where the editor, the good Robin Anderson, told me I could stay until I was seventy. Another divorce, and another change of home, edged me out of the profession and into early retirement. Looking back on it all, I cannot better, but can add to, the late Nicholas Tomalin's classic summing-up: 'The only qualities essential for real success in journalism are rat-like cunning, a plausible manner and a little literary ability – plus knowing when to steal other people's phrases and ideas.' My two additions to that list are a mastery of the telephone and an aptitude for dodging impossible assignments. Those skills are best demonstrated in two anecdotes given to me by Ronald Harker, former night editor of the *News Chronicle* and the last of many generous contributors to this book. Both stories feature his friend, reporter Stuart Gelder. First, the telephonic tale, as told by Harker:

Gelder was an exceptionally able telephone interviewer, adapting his manner from the wheedling to the magisterial as occasion demanded. I recall one episode when the liner *Queen Mary* was running trials after a refit and, for some reason, Cunard forbade any communication between ship and shore. Gelder put in a personal call to the ship's cat. When the telephone operator giggled he sternly reminded her that, under Post Office regulations, the only reason for refusing it was if the prospective interlocutee had declined to receive such a call. Had the ship's cat done so? She put the call through. The captain picked up the phone and was almost choking with exuberance because the liner had apparently broken most of the speed records in the book. He poured out the whole story and the paper had an exclusive. It was, I think, headlined Mary Queen of Knots.

Now for Harker's account of the artful dodger:

It happened in Gerald Barry's time as editor of the *News Chronicle*, a year or so before the Edward VIII abdication crisis. The news editor summoned Gelder and told him he had heard that the then Prince of Wales was keeping a popsie down at Fort Belvedere. 'Go and check it out,' he ordered. Gelder, then new and green from Nottingham, was in despair. His unhappiness was spotted by a kindly old hand, Clepham Palmer, the parliamentary correspondent. He took Gelder out for a coffee at the Kardomah and told him: 'There's only one way to handle an assignment like this. There's a golf course not far from Belvedere. Go down there, pay a green fee, borrow a set of clubs from the pro and play a leisurely round. Then order a good lunch in the clubhouse and, if you feel like it, play another round. In any case, don't come back to the office until evening. Make out a generous expense sheet, tell the news editor you've made exhaustive enquiries and there's nothing in the story.' In some trepidation Gelder did this. When he confronted the news editor, his boss spared him hardly a glance as he said: 'I knew there was nothing in it. Barry picks up these daft tales in the Savoy grill.'

That was the Street, that was – or at least the funny side of it.